THE HEALING TOUCH

OF

AFFIRMATION

A book of reflections

THE HEALING TOUCH OF AFFIRMATION

THOMAS A. KANE, PH.D., D.P.S.

FOREWORD BY JAMES P. MADDEN

AFFIRMATION BOOKS

WHITINSVILLE, MASS.

To my friend
Anna Polcino

who shows me how well
intelligence and compassion can affirm.

CONTENTS

FOREWORD

This is what we proclaim to you: what was from the beginning, what we have heard, what we have seen with our eyes, what we have looked upon and our hands have touched — we speak of the word of life . . . 1 John 1:1

The words of St. John, evangelist, speak eloquently of what this inspiring book attempts. Father Thomas A. Kane, psychotherapist, educator, priest and a deeply human person, proclaims a message of faith, hope and love — a message of good news. It is not a complete message; it is confined to what he and others with whom he shares his life have heard, have seen with their eyes, have looked upon and have touched with their presence — that healing touch of affirmation.

The experience Father Kane is speaking of comes from a very special psychotheological community questing for communion with God and with man. This residential, therapeutic community is composed of both men and women, religious professionals. Living in this climate of concern and redemptive healing, Father Kane and others hear men and women cry out in agony and emotional turmoil and gradually hear them sing out in peace and freedom. He has seen men and women appear as dead, as bound with chains of despair and self-hatred; and he has seen them later appear as alive, as lights of hope reflecting a love for themselves and others. He has touched those trembling with fear and coldness and has touched them with the vibrations of love and outstretched arms of concern and deep compassion. It is from these living experiences that Father Thomas Kane has put to print a book that contains words of life for all who read its pages.

A theme which seems to be articulated on each page is that once said by our Lord: "I have come that you may have life and have it more abundantly," here and now, life in its many aspects, despite the opposition and hopelessness all around you, and the weaknesses within you. Man is to live now — fully, richly, divinely. Toward that end this book is written. It deals with the few basic things man needs for his wholeness and his holiness.

This is the psychotheological approach. The approach urges man to find in the integral acceptance of Christianity the highest accomplishment of his humanity — the nature of Christian experience — that experience which first came into being nearly two thousand years ago and which has been sustained ever since. It is hardly a cultural accident that questions concerning the nature of this experience should come before our eyes so vividly and inescapably at the present moment of history. For "experience" has become a central concept in modern-day life. People want to know how to feel, how to see, how to listen; how, in brief, to experience themselves, the material world, the reality of other people, the culture which surrounds them. They want to reach bed-rock and they believe that experience provides the tools with which to dig. It is precisely this experience and this life adventure Father Kane articulates so effectively in this book.

In working with the very ordinary material of human relationships, with the experience of people who express love, who express anger, who desire, Father Kane tries to show the reader the psychotheological cutting-edge of these relationships — what they reveal of the human condition and what they point to as central in that condition. Even more, he tries to show us how much we have lost by neglecting to see the importance of human transformation. For, at the deepest level, a person who is enlightened by his experience, who begins to see patterns and pointers, is a person on the way to transformation, toward a wholesome image of God and himself.

With brilliant persuasiveness and insight, Father Thomas A. Kane reflects that affirmation, rather than rigid formation, provides the key to Christian growth and development. It is to enter into community, to discover who we are in relationship to other human beings. It is with this affirmation and in community with "significant others" that we discover who we are. This Christian self-discovery is experienced in peace and ever-enriching growth.

Father Kane's sensitivity and deep awareness of these profound realities challenges the reader to reflection, reevaluation and possibilities of inner discoveries of self and others who touch his life so deeply. May his sharing of himself, his thoughts, his experiences, touch you with the healing touch of affirmation as it has so often touched me in many ways he will never fully know.

James P. Madden, C.S.C.
Stonehill College
North Easton, Massachusetts
May 1, 1976

PREFACE

This is a slim volume of *reflections* concerning the psychotheology of affirmation. It makes no claim to have all the answers; it does have some.

Much more could have been written about each topic contained in this book. My intention is to be brief. My hope is that the reader will be moved to pause, consider, and reflect upon what is presented herein. In sharing these reflections, I desire to aid the reader to discover his or her own potential which brings about a creative and authentic response to life. Cardinal Suenens speaks succinctly when he states: "The greatest good we do to others is not to give them of our wealth but to show them their own."

Many persons spend most of their time living in the scared past or threatening future. Few live in the present moment. This book is another invitation to live in the present moment. The present offers happiness, health and the possibility of affirmation.

It is not my intention to repeat what I have acknowledged elsewhere. I wish to present these reflections coming from my experience as a Christian priest who knows and feels the affirmation of other human beings and the beautiful peace that compels me to accept Christ as brother and Savior.

With fondness, I recall the many requests of my students, clients, and parishioners to put my reflections in writing. I do hope this "significant little" will enable and encourage others to greater depths of reflection and articulation of the psychotheology of affirmation.

In this book I have drawn inspiration from many sources, and I am grateful to all of them. My total thank-you list is too long to be mentioned here. A few persons must be acknowledged. I continue to appreciate Sister Anna Polcino, nun-physician-psychiatrist and Founder of the House of Affirmation to whom this book is dedicated on the 25th Anniversary of her Religious Profession of Vows. I am indebted to my brother-priest, James P. Madden, C.S.C., for teaching me much about gentleness by his manner of living.

I am thankful to Edward Fish for the paintings he shares with us; to Father Thomas Schmied, O.F.M. Cap., who did all the photography work in this book; and to Sister Lynn Conroy, S.C., Ph.D., who did the proof reading. I am most appreciative to my assistants, Ghislaine P. Parenteau and William E. Ashe, Jr.; their patience with me is a special gift of God. I continue to remember with affection, all staff and residents, present and former, of the House of Affirmation, International Therapeutic Center for Clergy and Religious.

The Lord has blessed my life with a good family and loyal friends — significant others who continually and freely offer me their *healing touches of affirmation*. To these great companions, I offer in thanksgiving and as a *gift* the words of the medical philosopher, Felix Marti-Ibanez, M.D.:

> Every man goes through life shielding his individual smallness behind a majestic group of giants whom he chooses as life companions. This august

and mighty troupe is acquired sometimes all at once, sometimes in the course of years. The choice of such peerless companions is made because their personality charms us, their life inspires us, or their word enlightens us. Sometimes we have had the good fortune to know them personally; more often we come to know them through their work, their speeches, writings, thoughts, and example. But maybe it is not we who choose them to accompany us on life's journey; maybe it is they who from their exalted place reach down to adopt us, even as the sun in its journey across the heavens chooses to mirror itself in the humble waters of a brooklet.

Thomas A. Kane

Fear not that life *should come to an end,*

but rather fear that it should never

have a beginning.

— John Henry Cardinal Newman

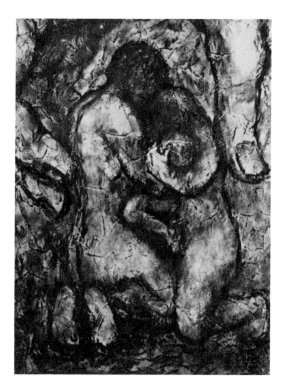

chapter one

AFFIRMATION IS CREATION

God created me when his purpose first unfolded,
before the oldest of his works.
I was by his side, a master craftsman,
delighting him day after day,
ever at play in his presence
at play everywhere in his world
delighting being with mankind.

— Proverbs 8:22-23, 30-31

The Painting

The reproduction of the painting on the cover of this book is no accident nor is it there as a gimmick to sell the book. The title of the painting is "Creation,"[1] by the contemporary American artist, Edward Fish.

Look at this painting, pause, appreciate, take delight in it. Know and feel its gentleness, its strength, its tenderness, its beauty and truth. This painting is not busy nor hurried; its concern is with *being* and not primarily with doing. Notice that the hand of God touches gently the soft bodies of man and woman, and they in turn, in tender embrace, cuddle their baby. This painting will enchant you. Reflect on "Creation" and you will feel at least the stirrings of affirmation within your mind and heart.

The Artist

Not long ago I visited the artist whose painting I had admired for years. To my delight, I found a man not concerned with *producing* paintings, as are so many others in his scenic seaport town of Rockport, Massachusetts. His studio revealed him to be a veritable adventurer in the realm of art. He paints in all mediums and all styles, ranging from realism to abstraction. The artist was not hurried, happy to be with me for conversation and appreciation of his works. "Many people look, but few see or perceive," the artist spoke with a note of sadness in his voice.

The artist spoke softly of his painting, "Creation," and said that he wishes to express in this painting the nobility of family life as the greatest of the Lord's creation. He spoke with pride of his wife, his three daughters, and their *home* as the values he hoped others might come to appreciate from his art. I met his lovely wife and shared brewed tea with them.

Edward Fish is an affirmer of goodness. He does not prostitute himself with functionalism nor has he given himself over to utilitarian values. He paints the beauty of family and the simple things of life. Not a particularly religious man, I found him to be sensitively Christian and in search of a way of life uncontrolled by the faceless machine of technology which forces mankind into a predetermined mode. Another of his paintings, of his daughter, entitled "Amy With a Fishbowl," appears elsewhere in this book.

Great Teachers

It is with happiness that I write that I most often

find the truths of human behavior best taught, not in psychology or theology textbooks alone, but where all great insights concerning mankind have been found for centuries, in poetry, novels, music, art, the writings of philosophers, and in the biographies of great men and women and not so great men and women. These affirmers of mankind teach and heal us with their tender touches.

Alexander Solzhenitsyn in his Nobel Lecture of 1970 challenges the contemporary person to learn from significant teachers: "Will not Dostoevsky's words, 'The world will be saved by beauty,' turn out to be no slip of the tongue, but a prophecy? For he was granted extraordinary vision, he was amazingly inspired . . . And then perhaps art and literature will be able to help the modern world."[2]

Josef Pieper

Now we turn our attention to Josef Pieper, contemporary German philosopher. Forty-two years ago, when he was a twenty-eight year old professor, Pieper wrote a small book, *About Fortitude,* in the face of National Socialism — The Nazis. Today he has given us the best book available concerning the theory of affirmation. Rich in Thomistic anthropology and conversant with contemporary phenomenology, *About Love* is a penetrating study that I recommend for your careful and reflective reading.

It is from Pieper that we learn that creation is synonymous with affirmation. God calls us into being. This act of creation is the primal act of affirmation. "The most marvelous of all things a being can do is *to be.*"[3] It is God who in the act of creation affirms mankind: "I will that you exist . . . and it is very good that you exist." (Gen. 1:31) Because God delights in our being, we humans can dare to take delight in loving and affirming our brothers and sisters, and all of created things. There is no such thing as illegitimacy in God's plan. All that is called into being, all of creation is meant to reflect the goodness of God. Human nature is the greatest of God's creations and His love transforms all that is created. "God with His love neither destroys nor changes nature, but *perfects* it," Pius XII states so beautifully.

Brothers and Sisters Affirm

Happiness comes to persons who do not try to stand arrogantly before their Creator. Happiness comes to persons who celebrate their existence as the gift of God. But beyond existence, and acknowledgment that it is good that I am created by God, we need our brothers and sisters to make explicit the affirmation. "It is *good* that you are; how *wonderful* that you are you! In other words being created by God actually does not suffice, it would seem; the fact of creation needs continuation and perfection by the creative power of human love."[4] Over and above sheer existence, we need to be loved by another human person, *a significant other*. We are given meaning and strength by the affirmation of our parents, our brothers and sisters, our spouses, our friends, colleagues, and superiors.

Affirmation

The word affirmation comes from the Latin *affirmare* and means to make firm, to give strength to, to make strong. It implies assent, agreement, consent, a willingness to say "Yes" to all creation.

Affirmation is the acceptance of the goodness of the other person as he is. At the essence of all maturing love is affirmation: "You are good." "You are wonderful." The most tender, indeed healing, touch of affirmation is that I allow the other person to be as he is, immaturity and shortcomings included. I do so not out of fear but out of free choice. I encourage the other to be who he is so that his potential may be realized.

The psychology of affirmation, or creation, goes beyond the utilitarianism so often found in the Western world. Affirmation is concerned with being and not primarily with doing; it is not concerned with functionalism.

Notice that affirmation reflects the goodness of a person to himself. You are good because you are you; because you have great worth being your unique self. You are God's creation! Good, not primarily because you have done anything, or accomplished a great deal, or proven that you are successful; no, just because you are you! Once known and once felt, this is the healing touch of affirmation.

Martin Buber

The Jewish philosopher, Martin Buber, one of the earliest great persons to teach us about affirmation, writes: "In human society, at all levels, persons affirm one another in a practical way, to some extent or other, in their personal qualities and capacities, and society may be termed human in the measure to which its members affirm another.

"The basis of man's life with man is twofold: and it is one — the wish of every man to be affirmed as what he is, even as what he may become, by men; and the innate capacity in man to affirm his fellow-man in this way. That this capacity lies so immeasurably fallow constitutes the real weakness and questionableness of the human race; actual humanity exists only where this capacity unfolds. On the other hand, of course, an empty claim for affirmation, without devotion for being and becoming, again and again, mars the truth of life between man and man.

"Men need, and it is granted to them, to affirm one another in their individual being by means of genuine meetings; but beyond this they need, and it is granted to them, to see the truth, which the soul gains by its struggle, lights up to others, in a different way and even so be affirmed."[5]

Radical View of Humanity

We can understand and live affirmation by slowing down, by saving ourselves from the frenzy of always doing; by living and pausing to gaze at the goodness of others. I state this not just in a sentimental way, but as the radical (radical comes from the Latin *radix* and means the *basic* or *root* of something) and essential lifestyle. Affirmation is not a technique; it is an approach to living.

Ways of Affirmation

Ways of affirmation differ, but all are important. Affirmation can be *visual,* e.g. a responsive smile; *tactile,* e.g. an embrace; *auditory,* e.g. an expression of sympathy; and it can be *spiritual,* e.g. shared prayer. All ways of affirmation lead our brothers and sisters to know and feel their own goodness and help them to gently live this life with happiness. Affirmation can only be given as a free gift and can only be a gift if it is graciously received by another person. Thomas Aquinas, over seven hundred years ago, stated that "love is the first gift. Whatever else is freely given to us becomes a gift only through love."

Affirmation of Things

The affirmed person not only affirms his brothers and sisters, but all that *is.* He affirms the dignity and nobility of being, as such. Thus, he can affirm goodness, even in a drop of water or in a blade of grass. Affirmation develops within mankind a sense of awe and reverence for all of creation.

Once we experience affirmation, we wish to share it with others and have an "inner readiness," as the French philosopher Gabriel Marcel puts it, to accept affirmation when and where offered to us, individually or corporately.

Jan Cardinal Alfrink

Bernard Jan Alfrink, the then Cardinal Archbishop of Utrecht, in a speech in Whitinsville, Massachusetts, stated: "We find that non-Christian people are often irritated by the fact that Christianity calls itself the religion of love, while at the same time it has not succeeded in building up much of a real *communio* not even in its own circles. Marxism rebukes Christians for always talking about God and about love, while forgetting at the same time to make the world a place worth living in for everyone. And who would dare to say that Christians could justly ignore this rebuke without even making the beginning of an examination of conscience?

"Perhaps the problem could be posited this way, that the world today is honestly dissatisfied with religion as it presents itself and rightly asks of religion to be taken seriously by the Church. Very often the world of today experiences the religious person as one who is not happy himself and does not make others happy. To the world the religious person resembles the famous Prometheus of Greek mythology. Chained immovably to a rock, bound, not free, and tortured by an eagle picking at his liver, he suffered interior pains, division, uncertainty, dissatisfaction, intolerance. . . . It could be very interesting and at the same time instructive to see how often in the

Scriptures the word 'joy' is written and used as a kind of label for the Christian. 'I have spoken thus to you, that my joy may be in you, and that your joy may be complete.' In human intercourse it is always the human being who gives joy and happiness to the other. It is the Christian who should take first place in this art of affirming his fellowman. But he who wants to affirm his fellowman will have to be affirmed himself first by someone else. Only the one who has blossomed out in affirmation is able to open up and affirm the other. It is not difficult to see how so many people are asking to be affirmed by someone else: the man who is lonely for whatever reason, or the man in the midst of an identity crisis who no longer recognizes himself and is uncertain of himself. To affirm and to be affirmed is a matter of fundamental interaction in human society. One who has not been affirmed by others is not able to affirm others. He will soon deny the other in the futile hope of improving his own situation through self-affirmation."

Bold Thinking

It is evident from what has been said thus far that there is required much more new and bold thinking if we are to meet the challenge of the future. Affirmation can affect the future; it does not, however, seek to control; it is like the sun upon the rose bringing it to blossom.

Having been affirmed by another and affirming others, I will know and feel who I am; I will have a true identity. I will sense that I am different but acceptable; that I belong in the world and that I am contributing to it and can change it; that there is a unique place for me and that I have a unique contribution; that I can choose freely to love and to do; that I cannot be ultimately destroyed. I am confidently open to what is to come.

In this first chapter we have viewed what affirmation is from a point of health, not what affirmation is not, or the symptoms of the non-affirmed person. The approach of affirmation is far from complete unless one reflects on "the significant other" and the tragedy of the opposite of affirmation, deprivation and denial. We will, in subsequent chapters, attempt to reflect on these and other matters.

Summary

Thus, we have briefly reflected on affirmation. We know that the words affirmation and creation are synonymous, even inter-changeable. We have briefly reflected that affirmation is concerned with being and not primarily concerned with a person's accomplishments. We accept a person's being and we affirm our human loves when we convey, "I love you as you are, because you are." We have stated also that God first affirmed us prior to our *doing* anything, and this very affirmation makes all of our brothers and sisters lovable. The other person knows and feels our love without doing anything.

chapter two

WHAT IS HEALING?

Love is the 'affirmative of affirmatives';
it enlarges the vision,
expands the heart.
Love is the dove of peace,
the spirit of brotherhood;
it is tenderness and compassion,
forgiveness and tolerance.
Love is the dynamic motivation
behind every worthy purpose;
it is the upward thrust
that lifts men to the heights.
The art of love is God at work through you.

— Anonymous

Francis MacNutt's book, *Healing,*[6] is probably one of the most widely read contemporary resources for Christians in regard to the healing ministry. In his Preface, MacNutt states that at "a house in Whitinsville, Massachusetts" he became convinced that the healing ministry should become normal work for all Christians. It is interesting to note that I now sit and write in the very *same* home, ten years later. We have never met personally, but I am sure this house has and is a place where one knows and feels a presence that can only be called Divine. Though no longer the School of Pastoral Care, this house continues the ministry of healing as an international therapeutic center for clergy and religious — The House of Affirmation.

I have come to respect MacNutt through his writings and because of the good words people have for him. I have clinically seen some of the results of his ministering to persons resulting in significant healing of emotional problems. He is a special gift of God with his rich influence in the charismatic renewal.

A Definition

I neither hope nor want to duplicate what MacNutt has already stated about healing. But for the purpose of this present book I wish to devote some reflections on "healing" as pertinent to the approach of affirmation. For me, *healing is a satisfactory response to a crisis made by a group of people both individually and corporately.* This definition is important if we are going to have a meaningful reflection. The definition contains no specific medical or theological word barriers. Thus, physicians, nurses, therapists, social workers, probation officers, clergy, religious, theologians, and even the so-called "ordinary person" can respond to it. All of our brothers and sisters are participants in healing.

A Response to Crisis

Healing is a response to a crisis — a satisfactory response, *enough* of a response. The word crisis is often used in a special sense in the New Testament. It comes from the Greek "krisis" and is frequently translated as "judgment." Healing, then, is a judgment we make in response to a decisive moment in the life of our brother or sister; it is a challenge situation, and either we respond or we do not. But, either way, we have made a judgment. Healing is a judgment we make and it is an opportunity to respond to the Gospel. It is an opportunity for us to react creatively and to reach new levels of maturity.

Contemporary Christians are rediscovering the power of healing through Jesus Christ. The approach to healing is through affirmation. Michael Scanlan, in his popular book, *Inner Healing,* reminds us that the Christian "who seeks to serve with the heart of Jesus — as a wounded and healed sinner, celebrating the gift of the peace of Christ, relying on the love of Jesus to work through him, and acting in the name of Jesus in conjunction with other members of the Body — will thereby follow certain general patterns. His approach will be one of affirmation in love and truth; he will therefore always reflect an affirmation of and a love for the true good that is in the person. He will always be good news more than bad news."[7]

Jesus Heals by Affirmation

Affirmation makes *firm,* gives *strength,* and heals our brothers and sisters of their wounds. Jesus, the Divine Physician, *healed* by affirming mankind. The New Testament celebrates examples of Jesus healing by affirming men and women in gentle ways. He so much wanted his followers to be in peace, to take delight in his presence. He wanted his followers to share in creation, to be thinkers of their thoughts and feelers of their feelings, rather than just doers. As a matter of fact, Jesus was repelled by the "busy-ness" in his Father's temple, and by the futility of the "doing-rules" of the Pharisees.

Reflecting on the Scriptures we find many examples of Jesus' healing touch of affirmation. The Scottish biblical scholar, William B. Stevenson, as early as 1910, presented a reflection on the meaning of affirmation as used in both the Old and New Testament, and as understood by our consideration of the word in this present book.

Jesus healed many wounds of anxiety, of unhappiness, of low self-esteem, frustration, etc. We will cite a few examples of Jesus as he goes about affirming persons. The reader is encouraged to take Scripture in hand and reflect on the many affirmations of the lovableness of humanity as taught by Jesus, the Divine Physician.

An Affirmed Criminal

Even while he was being crucified, Jesus affirmed the criminal on the cross who asked Him for remembrance: "One of the criminals hanging there abused him. 'Are you not the Christ?' he said. 'Save yourself and us as well.' But the other spoke up and rebuked him. 'Have you no fear of God at all?' he said. 'You got the same sentence as he did, but in our case we deserved it: we are paying for what we did. But this man has done nothing wrong. 'Jesus,' he said, 'remember me when you come into your kingdom.' 'Indeed, I promise you,' he replied, 'today you will be with me in paradise.' (Luke 23:39-43)[8]

An Affirmed Tax Collector

One of the most profound scriptural illustrations of the meaning of affirmation is found in the account of the meeting of Jesus with Zacchaeus, the tax collector. Neither accepted nor loved, Zacchaeus desires to be accepted by others simply for being himself. Such acceptance he had not known, and he evidently placed some hope in Jesus of Nazareth. Jesus was to pass through his neighborhood and there would be a crowd to see him. As at other times, because of occupation and physical appearance, Zacchaeus would be denied again. Trying to get a view of Jesus, Zacchaeus — so small in stature — could not work his way through the crowd. He climbed a sycamore tree on the side of the road hoping to view the Nazarene. Jesus does not pass him by, but accepts him as he is. "Zacchaeus, come down because I must stay with you today," Jesus calls out to the little man in the tree. What is the result? Zacchaeus immediately is opened like a flower in bloom.

Zacchaeus stood there, and said to the Lord: "Here and now, I give away half of my possessions to charity, and if I have cheated anyone, I am ready to repay him four times over." (Luke 19:1-9)

An Affirmed Mother

Jesus affirmed both his mother and the anxious couple at the marriage reception at Cana. With tender love, he responded to her gracious request on their behalf. "Three days later there was a wedding at Cana in Galilee. The mother of Jesus was there, and Jesus and his disciples had also been invited. When they ran out of the wine provided for the wedding, the mother of Jesus said to him, 'They have no wine.' Jesus said, 'Woman, why turn to me? My hour has not come yet.' His mother said to the servants, 'Do whatever he tells you.' There were six stone water jars standing there, meant for the ablutions that are customary among the Jews; each jar could hold twenty or thirty gallons. Jesus said to the servants, 'Fill the jars with water,' and they filled them to the brim. 'Draw some out now,' he told them, 'and take it to the steward.' They did this; the steward tasted the water, and it had turned into wine. Having no idea where it came from — only the servants who had drawn the water knew — the steward called the bridegroom and said, 'People generally serve the best wine first, and keep the cheaper sort till the guests have had plenty to drink; but you have kept the best wine till now.' (John 2-1-11)

Affirmed Youngsters

He affirmed the little children when his apostles were ready to turn them away. "People were bringing little children to him, for him to touch them. The disciples turned them away, but when Jesus saw this he was indignant and said to them, 'Let the little children come to me; do not stop them; for it is to such as these that the kingdom of God belongs. I tell you solemnly, anyone who does not welcome the kingdom of God like a little child will never enter it.' Then he put his arms around them, laid his hands on them and gave them his blessing. (Mark 10:13-16)

An Affirmed Widow

He gave a new strength and a new sense of importance to the poor widow. "He sat down opposite the treasury and watched people putting money into the treasury, and many of the rich put in a great deal. A poor widow came and put in two small coins, the equivalent of a penny. Then he called his disciples and said to them, 'I tell you solemnly, this poor widow has put more in than all who have contributed to the treasury; for they have all put in money they had over, but she from the little she had has put in everything she possessed, all she had to live on.' " (Mark 12:41-44)

An Affirmed Woman

To the adulterous woman, Jesus "looked up and said, 'Woman, where are they? Has no one condemned you?' 'No one, sir,' she replied. 'Neither do I condemn you,' said Jesus, 'go away, and don't sin any more.' " (John 8:10-11)

An Affirmed Leader

Even though he had been denied three times, Jesus affirms Peter and gives him new strength. " 'But you,' he said, 'who do you say I am?' Then Simon Peter spoke up, 'You are the Christ,' he said, 'the Son of the living God.' Jesus replied, 'Simon son of Jonah, you are a happy man! Because it was not flesh and blood that revealed this to you but my Father in heaven. So I now say to you: You are Peter and on this rock I will build my Church. And the gates of the underworld can never hold out against it. I will give you the keys of the kingdom of heaven: Whatever you bind on earth shall be considered bound in heaven; whatever you loose on earth shall be considered loosed in heaven.' " (Matthew 16:16-20)

An Affirmed Son

In the parable of the Prodigal Son, Jesus pushes aside all rationalizations and functionalisms. "While he was still a long way off, his father saw him and was moved with pity. He ran to the boy, clasped him in his arms and kissed him tenderly. Then his son said, 'Father, I have sinned against heaven and against you. I no longer deserve to be called your son.' But the father said to his servants, 'Quick! Bring out the best robe and put it on him; put a ring on his finger and sandals on his feet. Bring the calf we have been fattening, and kill it; we are going to have a feast, a celebration, because this son of mine was dead and has come back to life; he was lost and is found.' And they began to celebrate." (Luke 15:20-25)

The Affirming Church

In all these actions and parables Jesus teaches us that the union of human persons creates an atmosphere for growth and healing. Jesus Christ whose Body is the

Church offers us, too, the gift of being affirmed members in love; in His Body we know a new dignity. The Church, rich in its tradition, ever fresh in its articulation, offers strength, nobility of being, and an opportunity for growth, healing and health. Our Christian understanding of the Mystical Body hits at the very essence of what the *scientiae humanae* seemingly are just discovering.

Healing and Society

The nun-surgeon-psychiatrist, Anna Polcino, has established healing communities in West Pakistan, Bangladesh, and, more recently, a psychotheological community in America. Lecturing to her medical students at the University of Massachusetts Medical School, Dr. Polcino states, "Healing is to be understood not only as an alleviation of external pressures but also as a response to man's search for internal liberation. Healing includes going to the root cause of manifested problems by helping bring about structural change; that is, by not letting change control us but by our controlling the forces of change, which aims at deeper personal liberation. It is the task to which redemptive incarnation addresses itself. In reality, healing is aimed at the development of people in authentic diversity, accepting the individual where he is, and thus, we can say, affirming that individual.

"Healing can be seen in the context of today's situation and the thrust toward liberation that embraces man's aspirations and that struggles to free man not only from personal bondage, but — even more important — from social bondage, from these products of our religio-cultural, political, economic system. Healing ministry includes everyone, whether professional or not, and it is a ministry that draws on the faith dimension of an individual's commitment and reaches out to the community and to the society in which the individual finds himself. Healing of the whole man implies the healing not only of the physical but the mental, as well, and it cannot be separated from other activities that in some way or other are aimed at restoring man to his physical or spiritual wholeness. All such activities, whether on the individual, social, political, national, or international level — all are interrelated. They all strive for man's liberation, which, in fact, is none other than the freedom from all bonds that prevent him from developing into the mature and free man that he was to be, by God's design, and for which he was re-created by Christ.

"Our strong desire should be affirming care to help restore man to his original wholeness and thus to contribute to his happiness. This means that we do not see persons as cases to be dealt with but as persons in need of our loving care."[9]

The Church professes and proclaims that its root and cornerstone is Incarnate Love. Yet, ironically, many Christians agonize because of a devastating lack of love in their lives. The Lord said, "Abide in my love . . . These things I have spoken to you, that my joy may be in you, and that your joy may be full." (John 15:10-11)

Why do so many Christians not feel this joy? Where is this healing touch of affirmation for those who feel inferior, uncertain, worthless and unloved?

chapter three

WHERE IS THIS TOUCH OF AFFIRMATION?

The shade of my tree
is for passers-by,
its fruit is for the one
for whom I wait.

— Tagore

When Helen Keller's teacher, Anne Sullivan, first met her student, she found a six-year-old girl who was blind, deaf and "uncontrollable as a wild animal." The little girl tyrannized her family; she would kick and bite if she did not get her own way. Anne Sullivan intuitively responded. Every time the little girl kicked her, she gave her a slap.

Was this behavior modification? Or cruelty? No; motherly affection and concern permeated all Anne's caring discipline. Later, when Helen Keller wrote her memoirs, the slaps were forgotten as she recalled that distant day when she met her beloved teacher for the first time. "I felt approaching footsteps, I stretched out my hand, as I supposed, to my mother. Someone took it, and I was caught up and held close in the arms of her who had come to reveal all things to me, and more than all things else, to love me." Anne Sullivan was the affirmer, the significant other, who created new life for Helen Keller.

The Futility of Reaching

If we stop for a moment and observe human behavior, we see contemporary men and women striving to win acceptance, indeed, many reaching out and pleading for affirmation. They are often, unknowingly, seeking it where it cannot be found and their search becomes despairing and futile. Trying to prove themselves to be worthwhile, they try to affirm themselves by doing many things and striving to achieve success for the sake of success. Many of these people seek affirmation in bed, switching partners, or seek affirmation in always trying to please people. They commonly think that job or sexual status will give them affirmation so they become work-a-holics or sex-a-holics. Often the futile searcher has personality traits that may display a false timidity, or arrogance in dominating others, a false joviality, compulsive perfectionism, "name dropping" behavior, rebellion against authority. Or such a person may become a do-gooder, never able to say 'no' or draw limits; a procrastinator; or one who is always putting himself down, or becoming the martyr or sufferer.

All of these ways can only lead to anger, unhappiness, futility and despair. We must repeat over and over again that affirmation cannot be grabbed for; we really cannot *do* things or perform behavioral tasks which will lead to our "winning" affirmation. Only another person can affirm us. The healing touch of affirmation comes primarily from another human being, that *significant other.*

Significant Other

The *significant other* is that beautiful human person who reflects my goodness back to me; that person who accepts me as I am and for who I am. The *significant other*, though aware of my shortcomings and immaturity, compels me to take joy in being myself and challenges my potential for growth and love. I know and feel that this other person loves me and is not concerned with using me. From the significant other I grow emotionally in the essentials of affiirmation, i.e., trust, recognition, acceptance, appreciation and reverence for my own goodness. The significant other gives me strength, a sense of my own *firm*-ness, while not robbing me of my individuality. The significant other moves me with joy to sing out "alleluia"; "I am good and I am wonderful." Only through the known and felt affirmation of significant others, can a human mature in the joy of living. One who is consciously experiencing love can say, "I need you in order to be myself . . . In loving me you give me myself, you let me be."[10]

Stages of Development

A person grows in appreciation of self only through the affirmation of the significant others. All experts agree that the foundations of good emotional health are laid in early childhood and that a happy childhood and secure environment are important to growth and development. Frederick Leboyer, the French obstetrician, offers sustaining evidence to the aforementioned truths in his new best sellers, "Birth Without Violence" and "Loving Hands."

Let us sketch the presence of the significant others as follows:

DEVELOPMENTAL STAGE	SIGNIFICANT OTHERS
In the womb	The mother
Infancy	Mother primarily, and Father
Pre-school years	Parents, older brothers and sisters, relatives
Early school years	Same as above; but now enter other significant adults, e.g., teachers, clergymen, etc.
Adolescent years	Family closeness important; friends now affirm The Parental Proclamation: "You are you" "You are a worthwhile individual."
College years	Friends, other loves now affirm significantly.
Marriage	Two mature adults affirm one another.
Celibate style	Definite need to develop close emotional bonds with women and men friends.
Middle years	Husband, wife, friends, and children reflect back to parents their own goodness.
Retirement years	Husband, wife, children, and other caring persons

We have pointed to a person's need to be affirmed by a significant other in various stages of life. In chapter five, "The Denied Touch — Deprivation Neurosis," we will see the tragic result when a person has had little affirmation or no true significant other in his life.

Once again the importance of significant others in childhood cannot be underestimated. The family is the center of affirmation and it is here that the person first learns what he feels about himself and others. "The key to personal acceptance, to personal affirmation which is the pivot of physical and intellectual functioning lies in the unique experiences of the child in the hands of the most powerful affirmers, its parents, in the course of the early years."[11]

We see many adult men and women around us who never really had mature parents who could emotionally be *enough* for them as significant others. These men and women live in the world of the deprived and have common characteristics: feeling unwanted, lacking in self-esteem, finding it difficult to trust others, to give or receive loving feelings, and to initiate or maintain meaningful inter-personal relationships.

Many persons can be affirmed, even if they have been deprived in earlier life. This is why what I have written in previous chapters concerning affirmation takes on new significance. Many people will be affirmed and will grow emotionally if a mature, significant other enters their lives. Once you recognize your need for the significant other, then you should slow down, meet life with a sense of openness and expectancy. Your intuition (see chapter seven) will tell you who this significant other will be; this other human being who will be aware of your unique wonderfulness and goodness. You will not have to *do* anything, for the significant other will be attracted to you and take delight in you — the person's touch, smile, words, will literally begin to heal you and you will feel better.

In his book of essays, *Cycles of Affirmation,* Jack Dominian, M.D., writes: "The deepest layer of affirmation requires a relationship of trust and closeness in which the physical, psychological, intellectual, and social aspects of each are identified, encouraged to grow and affirmed by feelings which invest and maintain the total goodness of the person. In the very nature of the process, permanency in the forms of continuity, reliability and predictability are essential for the realization of the goal of affirmation."[12]

Affirmation Not Possession

Affirmation is a liberating experience both to the lover and to the beloved. Affirmation does not mean possession of the one I affirm. One of the most insightful reflectors of human experience today is John Powell, and in his recent book, *The Secret of Staying in Love,* he writes: "A sense of his own worth is no doubt the greatest gift we can offer to another, the greatest contribution we can make to any life. We can give this gift and make this contribution only through love. However, it is essential that our love be liberating, not possessive. We must at all times give those we love the freedom to be themselves. Love affirms the other as *other.* It does not possess and manipulate him as *mine.* Pertinent here is the quotation of Frederick Perls: 'You did not come into this world to live up to my expectations. And I did not come into the world to live up to yours. If we meet it will be beautiful. If we don't, it can't be helped.' . . . This means that wanting what is best for you and trying to

be what you need me to be can be done only in a way
that preserves your freedom to have your own feelings,
think your own thoughts, and make your own decisions.
If your personhood is as dear to me as my own, which
is the implication of love, I must respect it carefully and
sensitively. When I affirm you, my affirmation is based
on your unconditional value as a unique, unrepeatable
and even sacred mystery of humanity."[13]

Thus, we can see that the touch of affirmation comes
through another human being, *the significant other*, who
opens me to my own goodness and the goodness of all
creation. Having been affirmed by another, I will experience the Creator and the world with love, peace and joy.

We have taken John Henry Cardinal Newman's words
as the motto for this book: "Fear not that life will come to
an end, but rather fear that it will never have a beginning." For many persons there is a new birth, a new beginning, once they have discovered, been touched by, the
significant other and know and feel the delight of his or
her affirming care.

May I share a poem with you, written by the American poet, Grace Stricker Dawson, entitled: "To A
Friend".[14]

> You entered my life in a casual way,
>   And saw at a glance what I needed;
> There were others who passed me or met me each
> day,
>   But never a one of them heeded.
> Perhaps you were thinking of other folks more,
>   Or chance simply seemed to decree it;
> I know there were many such chances before,
>   But the others — well, they didn't see it.

You said just the thing that I wished you would
say,
    And you made me believe that you meant it;
I held up my head in the old gallant way,
    And resolved you should never repent it.
There are times when encouragement means such
a lot,
    And a word is enough to convey it;
There were others who could have, as easy as not—
    But, just the same, they didn't say it.

There may have been someone who could have done
more
    To help me along, though I doubt it;
What I needed was cheering, and always before
    They had let me plod onward without it.
You helped to refashion the dream of my heart,
    And made me turn eagerly to it;
There were others who might have (I question that
part)
    But, after all, they didn't do it!

Jesus — The Significant Other

Jesus is God's divine-human affirmation of mankind;
and he is at the same time our "amen" to God. (2 Cor.
1:19). "The New Testament, however, does not look
merely to Jesus Christ for the solution to man's problems of loving. It encourages us to look through Christ
to the Godhead. Christ made his central moral exhorta-
tion to men that they must love. In doing this he was
revealing the nature of man to men, and behind that the
nature of God to men. Jesus' importance was not only
what he was in himself, perfect Man, but that he was
the Word of God, too, an explanation of God to men."[15]

Ultimately the fullness of affirmation will be found "in him, through him and with him," the Significant Other! Prayer, the language of awareness, brings us to relationship with the Savior of whom Paul writes to the Church at Corinth, "Before anything was created, he existed and he holds all things in Unity."

Affirmation, as previously noted, is the awareness that I am intrinsically good, and is my acceptance of this fullness of my being. Jesus could affirm others because there was nothing within himself of which he was not aware or would not accept; thus, he could be aware of all other people and he needed to reject nothing but sin.

A new vision of the Church as Mystical Body emerges when we are affirmed persons and *live* affirming others, because we are intimately in the presence of the most Significant Other, Jesus the Christ. We are encouraged in Paul's prayer to the Church at Ephesus that "he may live in your hearts through faith, and then planted in love and built on love, you will with all the saints have the strength to grasp the breadth and the length, the height and the depth, until knowing the love of Christ, which is beyond all knowledge, you are filled with the utter fullness of God." (Eph. 3:17-19)

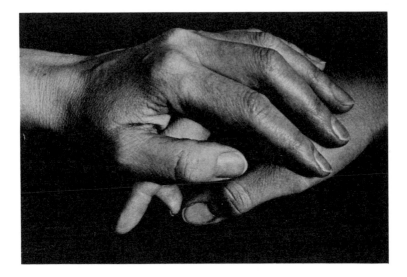

We do not need words.
 Our eyes speak
 our touch reveals
Each new day we discover new beauty
 in silence,
 of each other.

— Walter Rinder

chapter four

AFFIRMATION OF HUMAN DIGNITY IS HEALTH

Man lives by affirmation
even more than he does by bread.

— Victor Hugo

As a psychotherapist, I often go to "mental health" conferences only to find the agenda filled with topics such as schizophrenias, addiction, neuroses, etc., and I am at a loss to find any topic on health *per se*. Too often today our stress is on illness and not on health.

Michael Wilson of England, a priest and medical doctor, has written in his latest book, *Health Is For People*, that "to argue that health is more than meeting basic human necessities for food, clothing and shelter, is not to devalue these basic necessities . . . Health is not for the rich to give to the poor. Health is a quality of life they make together. Neither can possess health apart from the other; nor can one steal health from the other without robbing himself. Rich and poor, doctor and patient, oppressor and oppressed make one another healthy or unhealthy. Health is non-competitive.

"Nevertheless it is not just food, medicine and other materials which are shared. In some way, they are also the vehicle for human interchange. In sharing my loaf with another I may meet not only his hunger for food but also his hunger for a brother. Health is about sharing, sharing what we have with one another, sharing ourselves with one another. Health is about our relationship to material things, and our relationship to one another. We make health possible for one another."[16]

In the first three chapters of this book, we have reflected on affirmation from the viewpoint of health, not illness. We have seen that the affirmation of the person by the "significant other" person develops health. We can state quite declaratively that the affirmation of human dignity is health. However, we must view the development of health from four perspectives. By this we mean that a person needs to be healthy physically, intellectually, emotionally and spiritually.

Commonly, professionals in health care neglect or give little consideration to the highly significant emotional and spiritual aspects of man's nature. A person must mature in all four areas; the medical viewpoint that *neglects* man's spiritual aspect is *completely inadequate;* and society will never realize that it cannot solve the problems of mankind on a permanent basis, until it recognizes that void. I have found that much of the practice of humanistic medicine fails to appreciate the dimensions of faith; and that much of the practice of psychology either ignores the person's religious belief system because it is incompetent to handle it, or at worst considers it symptomatic of illness.

What Is Maturity?

Modern science and contemporary theology offer valuable insight into the constituents of maturity. I believe a mature person is an affirmed person and one who can affirm others. In the affirmed person, we see the healthy integration of the four maturities — physical, intellectual, emotional and spiritual. We see a person keen to spontaneity while responding to life truly and fully, happy with himself and others, and able to be quite effective in his work and play. The four maturities must be developed if a person is to be affirmed in a creative relationship with self, others, environment and God.

Affirmation is concerned with maturity. Affirmation helps develop the wholeness, the unique goodness of mankind's four maturities. Affirmation brings to blossom physical maturity, intellectual maturity, emotional maturity, and spiritual maturity. We shall consider briefly the four maturities in man's nature.

Physical Maturity

It is necessary that one feel affirmed about his body. That is, that others help us to know and feel comfortable about ourselves as "body" persons. No human person exists without a body. This may sound obvious, but my clinical practice has shown me that many persons suffer from a lack of felt-goodness concerning what their bodies are and how they look. All of us are unique in body appearance; no two are exactly alike. It is necessary that the *others* (see chart in chapter three) realize that their attitude toward the person they are affirming must include, if it is true affirmation, an increased awareness of his physical goodness.

It is sad to note that Western culture has produced a concern for the body that has not led to individual comfortableness with oneself as "body-person," but to a preoccupation with body as "sex-object," etc. We spend thousands of dollars during a lifetime on the physical aspect of life. Yet, ironically, if more people were affirmed, we would certainly see less physical illness.

Intellectual Maturity

The person must mature intellectually in order to be fully affirmed. We do not affirm a person if we do not encourage him to develop his intellectual capacities. This need not simply mean taking more schooling, but creating in him an attitude of delight in his intellect. Balance is important here. Our utilitarian philosophy of the past several hundred years has produced many intellectual giants, but left them emotional midgets.

Emotional Maturity

Much of the concern of this book is with a reflection of man's need to be affirmed emotionally. It is sufficient to repeat here that an affirmed person must *feel* that he is good and that he can relate to others with rich emotional investments which yield many dividends. He does not feel worthless or used if he is affirmed. He is assertive enough not to allow anyone or any process to treat him in such a manner. To possess the knowledge that I am loved is not sufficient; I must know and *feel* that I am loved if there is going to be happiness within the inner depth of my being.

Spiritual Maturity

There is a remarkable affinity between emotional and spiritual maturity. There can be no true affirmation if we do not affirm the goodness of the other as a reflection of the goodness of God. The affirmed person will take comfort and find peace in growth in the spiritual life. Once affirmed emotionally, spiritual maturation becomes a delight, not a hard grind or a painful set of rituals to be performed. Affirmed, knowing and feeling my own goodness, will bring me to a greater awareness of my *being;* and rich religious experience will be part of my daily life. Rather than presenting a threat to maturity, the spiritual life liberates and guarantees that I can be myself. The fact that God knows my name implies that he loves me: "Do not be afraid, for I have redeemed you; I have called you by name, you are mine. Because you are precious in my eyes, because you are honored and I love you." (Isaiah 43: 2, 4)

The fruits of the Spirit are very well enumerated by St. Paul: love, joy, peace, longsuffering, gentleness, goodness, faith, meekness, and temperance. (Galatians 5:22). These fruits are manifest in the life of the affirmed person. Affirmation is a state of inner radiance and healing presence. Spiritual maturity is for the affirmed person more than a series of techniques; it is the way of life in God, and its three essential elements are faith, hope and love, of which the greatest is love.

Summary

Briefly, we have reflected that mankind needs to find his affirmation in another human being and in the tender embrace of God. Further, we have reflected that to be affirmed one must mature physically, intellectually, emotionally, and spiritually. There is little dignity if a person feels he is living a life in the darkness of immaturity. Affirmation of human dignity produces maturity and health. Affirmation is the bread of life.

FEELINGS CYCLE OF AFFIRMATION

Healthy Feelings of Strength and *Firm*-ness

(If God and other people love me so much,
I must be worthwhile)

↑

Further Feelings of Affirmation
(Generally favorable response from others)

↑

Little Need to Escape
(Ability to be genuine and open with people)

↑

Assertive Behavior
(People cannot use me or walk over me)

↑

Self-acceptance
(Love of one's self)

↑

Feelings of my Own Goodness as Person
("I am good")

↑

Feelings of Affirmation by Significant Others

chapter five

THE DENIED TOUCH — DEPRIVATION NEUROSIS

*The strangers came and tried
to teach us their ways,
they scorned us just for being
who we are.*

Galway Bay — An Irish Ballad

Denial is the opposite of affirmation. Whether denial is directed toward one person, a group, or toward a social process, it usually is done with the attempt to control.

A Denied Wife

In his play, *Other People's Hearts*, Gabriel Marcel presents themes of a marriage in which we see the fundamental dynamics of denial, not affirmation. The husband more and more considers his wife as "part of himself" and denies her individuality. He takes her for granted, and presumes that his wishes are her wishes; he never discusses plans with her, or considers that she may have her own independent thoughts or feelings. She soon feels she is a thing used, not a person but a possession, and suffers deeply from this attitude of denial.

Deprived Students

Many of my students are caught up in trying to build

careers, with competitive spirits that try to get "to the top" no matter what or who may be the cost. The whole accent of their training (not education as properly understood) since they were young children has been on "What will you *do* to earn a living?" Little value is accorded to the question "What are you going *to be* as a person?" Persons are denied when the *only* reward offered them is how useful they will be doing a particular job, or performing a certain function in society.

If the child has not been loved for who he is, later on in life, no matter what position of honor or what achievement he attains, he will know and feel a sense of emptiness, worthlessness, and insecurity. Because of this denial, he may very well be a "doer" and an "achiever," but a very unhappy person; he may well be emotionally suffering from neurosis. Having achieved much, he may still be a person plagued by fear, anger, anxiety, distrust and depression.

A young child who enters a social system for education, treatment, or any other reason, should be accepted despite his errors, praised for his efforts, loved for who he is, and provided with persons worthy of emulation, if he is to internalize love of neighbor and God. A young child, like any other individual, does not mature by unnecessary criticism or by another's accentuating the negative in him. In fact, the one who denies is trying to attain fulfillment by controlling others to be like him. One denies 'the other' by constantly reminding him of his errors, his shortcomings, his immaturity, without first having loved the other for who he is.

Underdeveloped countries are denied advancement by economically powerful countries that try to control them by imposing on them their own cultural and spiritual values. Scientific progress has not led to man's fulfillment; often it has meant only denial. Many, in our age of "progress," are groping about bewildered and embittered by the forces that deny them, individually or corporately.

What Is Neurosis?

Briefly speaking, we can use "neurosis" as the name for unreasonable fears and excessive anxieties. Neurosis is fear repressing desire. A neurotic person goes through the day in touch with reality, but lives under the black cloud of mistrust, tension, and a lack of self-esteem.

Some signs of neurosis are:

1. *Anxieties* that have no visible cause . . . about vocation, family, occupation; a depressed, nagging feeling of being hopeless and helpless.
2. *Phobias* — exaggerated fears about persons, places or situations, e.g., fears of high places, open spaces, or closed rooms, etc.
3. *Compulsion* to do acts in a certain "perfect" way, e.g., if the routine is upset, so is the person.
4. *Physical complaints* — confusion of mind, frequent headaches, diarrhea, nausea, or persistent fatigue or listlessness.

The neurotic person is frightened by inter-personal relationships, often tries to escape from reality by refusing to make decisions, and suffers from extreme shyness. Often the neurotic believes no one likes him or could like him, is angry most of the time, makes trouble for himself and others. Many neurotics are "hoarders," i.e., they amass material things; the neurotic fear of others and their own selfishness make them unable to share time, money, or attention; but they demand these very things from other people.

Freud discovered that most neuroses start in childhood.

Other scientists have found that the neurotic can benefit from short-term treatment which helps minimize the fears and breaks the neurotic patterns of behavior, thus allowing the person to achieve a more emotionally rewarding life.

By the way, I do not believe that everyone is "a little neurotic." Neurosis is an emotional illness and only an integrated psychotherapist should attempt to diagnose and treat it. I do believe that we are all emotionally imperfect, but acceptance of imperfections is itself a part of good mental health.

Deprivation Neurosis

There are several kinds of neuroses. I believe that most persons lacking affirmation — who have been denied the touch of acceptance of who they are as persons — suffer from "deprivation," physically, intellectually, emotionally and spiritually. A notable lack of significant other, as discussed in chapter three of this book, is common to all deprivation neurotics. All deprivation neurosis is marked by a lack of maternal love, fear and repression of feelings. Denial, be it tactile, auditory, visual, or spiritual, results in an adult life characterized by an inability to establish normal emotional rapport, thus resulting in lack of friendships, excessive loneliness, failure in marriage and personal life.

Many deprivation neurotics do succeed in occupational and professional life. They are good "doers." Emotionally, they have intense feelings of low self-esteem and inadequacy. Feeling inferior to others, they try to compensate by trying to show others and themselves that they are important by having material possessions; seeking fame; controlling others through money, politics, physical force; or compulsively searching for adequacy in sexual expres-

sion, usually erratic homosexuality or compulsive heterosexual behavior. Realistically, we can call these persons
the victims of denial; they are the deprived who become
somewhat like T. S. Eliot's *Hollow Men*:

> Leaning together
> Headpiece filled with straw. Alas!
> Our dried voices
> ... Are quiet and meaningless
> As wind in dry grass
> Or rats' feet over broken glass
> In our dry cellar.

History is crammed with personalities who were cham-
pions in sports or intellectually gifted, but these very
persons have become depressed, unhappy, addicted to
alcohol, etc.

Therapy

At times, it is necessary that a person must enter therapy with a professional psychotherapist in order to seek
resolution of the neurotic conflict he may find evidenced
in his life. This is especially true of the deprivation neurotic. The significant other is important; and, I believe, at
times, *is* the primary healer in regard to the deprivation
neurotic. Other times, professional therapeutic interven-
tion is necessary.

It is important to enter into conversation with a therapist who works well with his own professional colleagues,
and who understands and appreciates varieties of life-
styles. There are plenty of "professional lovers" around
who will offer loving and healing for a high price. A person should go to a therapist who has personal integrity
and enjoys a good reputation among persons concerned
with religious values.

The value system of the therapist *does influence* the

therapeutic outcome. The therapist's value system is more important than his religious affiliation. At one time I would only refer persons to Catholic therapists, but experience has taught me that there are many good therapists of other persuasions. There are some Catholic therapists to whom I would never make a referral. The important ingredient in looking for a therapist is that he respects the client's rights of self-determination, life-style, etc. Remember, much of the practice of psychology either ignores the person's religious belief system because it is incompetent to handle it; or, at worst, considers it symptomatic of illness.

The remarkably gifted priest-psychotherapist, Dr. Adrian van Kaam, reflects: "My client, limited at first by his neurotic controls, after a period of therapy, reaches the fullness of freedom and is able to affirm himself as a source of initiative within his life situation. . . . The therapeutic relationship is fructifying and creative because therapeutic care creates a new "you" in the patient. Its aim is not to fashion a person in accordance with one or the other theory of personality, but to help bring about a free, unique person who will then feel, think, and act as an "I" and not as a disciple of any school of psychology or psychiatry. The force of my authentic, therapeutic love and concern leads to the moment in which anxiety-evoking situations lose their insurmountability for my client."[17]

An affirming therapist will convey more than just words or clichés to the deprivation neurotic. The affirming therapist will help provide an *experience* in which the neurotic sufferer will gain insight and will begin to grow in awareness of his own felt goodness. "There is, then, a basic affirmation to self-excellence that one needs to achieve in oneself and see reflected and confirmed by others. It is, therefore, an *affirmation-confirmation* personality need. Tempered and contained within the insightful awareness of a man's realization of his own limits, this, apparently, is his strongest source of meaning and value. It is at the heart of his courage to be and become. This is basic also to the way he regards others, since he tends to love them or disregard them according to the model of his attitudes towards himself."[18]

Deprivation Neurosis and Freedom

It is quite evident that the deprivation neurotic suffers from an unhealthy guilt and experiences much anxiety concerning his behavior. It should be stated that often there is little moral responsibility for some of the behavior of the deprivation neurotic because he suffers from an emotional illness and immaturity.

There certainly are limitations on the freedom of the deprivation neurotic because of the anxiety, the neurotic conflict itself, and because most neurotic problems are repressed in the unconscious, though the neurotic suffers from an awareness of his undesirable behavior. In his book, *The Individual and His Religion*, Gordon Allport writes: "Yet how can the neurotic sufferer, whose conduct is involuntary and whose impulses are prompted by mental tangles, the nature of which is largely unknown to him, be held accountable for conduct that he consciously deplores?"

Balance is important, however. To state that there is no evidence of freedom in the person with neurosis, as many scientists would say, is to further deny the neurotic. Not all acts of the sufferer are neurotic acts and many times the insights offered in psychotherapy open the door to new freedom.

In the healing process it is important for the deprivation neurotic that he be affirmed physically, intellectually, emotionally and spiritually. Affirmation breaks the barrier of neurotic entanglements and frees the person to understand what Jesus meant when he answered the scribe: "You must love the Lord your God with all your heart, and with all your soul, and with all your mind. This is the greatest and the most important commandment. The second, most important commandment is like it: You must love your neighbor *as yourself.*"

Thus, it appears that proper love of self is the model for love of others. Many times, neurotic sufferers will have to surrender some of the behaviors they dislike about themselves to God; they will learn that God can tolerate their immaturities. St. Therese of Lisieux seems to suggest this when she writes: "If you are willing to bear serenely the trial of being displeasing to yourself, you will be to Jesus a pleasant place of shelter."

Leisure
      means long moments of inner silence
      when nothing is said and
      nothing is done.
Leisure
      is neither recreation
      nor laziness
      it is expectation.

                    — Josef Pieper

chapter six

INTUITION AND AFFIRMATION

The mind is not a vessel to be filled
but a fire to be kindled.

— Plutarch

Did you ever say, "I have a hunch"? Of course you have; but you may have been trained to be suspicious of "hunches." Everyone has had this human experience. When a sudden discernment about someone or something has crossed one's mind, more often than not the insight proved to be accurate, popping into our consciousness, seemingly from nowhere. We *just know* the judgment to be accurate. Possibly, we minimize the experience by saying we were just good at "guessing." This explanation casually allows you to dismiss one of the most remarkable mental faculties, namely *intuition.*

What Is Intuition?

We define intuition as that faculty of the mind that apprehends truth directly, an *immediate* knowing without deduction or reasoning. Intuition is a single term that can represent scientific genius, poetic insight, ethical conscience and, in certain ways, religious faith. Intuition immediately makes known to us the opportunity for affirming the goodness of others and the goodness of things.

Carl Jung, one of the pioneers in the science of psychology, calls intuition a phenomenon by which a person can see beyond the facts, and perceive intangibles in a given situation. Viewing intuition as a dynamic source in life, Jung writes, "My psychological experience has shown time and again that certain contents arise from a psyche that is more complete than consciousness. They often contain a super-analysis or insight or knowledge which consciousness has not been able to produce. We have a suitable word for such occurrences — intuition."[19]

The Brain

Though it only weighs two and one-half pounds, the human brain stores incalculable amounts of information. Everything that an individual experiences is recorded in the mind. However, the conscious mind can recall only about ten per cent of this huge amount of data. The remaining ninety per cent lies buried in the unconscious. Under proper conditions, the subconscious can recall things that the person has long since forgotten and push them into consciousness. Henry Ford's revolutionary production theories are largely the product of intuition. Ford wrote that these ideas seemed "self-evident" to him; while, to his contemporaries, they were a radical surprise.

Cultivation of Intuition

Intuition is often referred to as a special gift of women; and we stereotype intuition in the same way we stereotype women, as sentimental and sloppy. No, intuition is a gift all persons have, regardless of sex, and it is no more "sentimental" than any other function of the intellect. It is important to acknowledge intuition and to develop it.

Louis Pasteur once remarked: "Intuition is given only to him who has undergone preparation to receive it." Intuition can be developed, but it requires cultivation just as much as the powers of thought, observation, and feeling.

How does one cultivate intuition? The following is suggested as a minimal way of cultivating this great faculty of the mind:

1. *Slow down, pause, stay still and just BE. Relax physically and mentally.* This is difficult in today's world surrounded as we are by continued noise and movement. Be silent. Silence can be a creative world in itself.

2. *Live in the present moment; it is the "now" that is important.* D. T. Suzuki, in *Buddhism in the Life and Thought of Japan*, observes, "Intuition takes time at its full value; it takes hold of each moment as it is born. Each moment is alive and significant. The frog leaps, the cricket sings, a dewdrop glitters, a breeze passes through the pine branches, and the moonlight falls on the murmuring mountain stream."[20]

3. *Look for intuition, believe in it and use it.* You can test intuition with your reason, realizing that physical instinct, prejudice and self-interest can, at times, appear disguised as intuition. However, a genuine flash of intuition is unmistakable. Trust your intuition; learn not to be suspicious of it.

4. *Allow yourself to laugh, to feel light and free.* Often laughter is an outward sign of an inner state of balance. Sri Krishna Prem, in *The Yoga of the Kathopanishad,* suggests: "Laughter was given by the Gods to man and it was one of their choicest gifts. No animal can laugh, nor does it need to since it lives in the harmony of the purely instinctive life. It is only man whose possession of an ego

introduces stresses and strains which cannot be avoided and for the healing of which, therefore, the Gods gave him the supreme gift. Time and again it will save us when otherwise all would be lost. He who cannot laugh, he whose devotions are too serious for the healing waves of laughter, had better look out: there are breakers ahead."[21]

5. *Encourage the intuitive faculty of your mind.* Remain attentive to the still small voice within you; have patience and be responsive. Undertake the inward journey. It is not made in space and time but in consciousness. A Hindu guru, defining the difference between Western and Oriental thinking, said that when a Westerner is presented with a problem, he says, "I will think my way through it"; whereas, the Hindu says, "I will try to raise my level of consciousness."

As a psychotherapist, I often encourage my clients to cultivate their intuition and to live accordingly. They report a new spontaneity and refreshment in living and doing. It is important to note that intuition cannot operate when the conscious mind is tied in knots or cluttered with worry and anxiety; relaxation is of prime importance.

Cultivated intuition leads to an immediate awareness of my own goodness and allows me to know the significant other when that person enters my life. Intuition is necessary to living a life of affirmation because it develops the person's sense of wonder, and enhances richness in the emotional life.

Religious Experience

When the intuitive faculty is trusted, lived, and cultivated, a person often will experience a direct realization of the soul's union with the divine. A person will know and feel the presence of the Godhead.

During the last days of his life, St. Thomas Aquinas experienced the fruition of cultivated intuition permeated by faith; he experienced a twofold ecstasy. His biographers share his experience with us in these words attributed to him: "Everything that I have written now seems like straw, by comparison with the things I have now *seen* and which have been revealed to me."[22]

chapter seven

THE ADVENTURE OF AMBITIOUS AFFIRMATION

If you have real love
you are inventive.
If you love
you try to find out,
you are interested.
If you really love
you are patient
you are long-suffering.
Certainly if you love
you accommodate yourself.
If you love
you want to give
you are tireless, selfless
and generous.
If you love
you really try to serve
and not just work.
One does not spare oneself
if one loves.

— Anna Dengel, M.D.

The preceding words are those of Anna Dengel, foundress of the Medical Mission Sisters. Fifty years ago, Anna Dengel founded this group of dedicated women to bring professional medical services to the underdeveloped countries — in particular, to the countries of the Moslem culture where women could not be seen by male doctors. Today there are seven hundred Sisters around the world who have followed in the footsteps of Anna Dengel as physicians, nurses, and educators participating in the healing ministry. The motivating force of her concern is affirmation — manifesting Christ's concern for the goodness of the *whole* human being.

Affirmation

Let us briefly repeat the steps of affirmation:
1. You exist.
2. It is good that you exist.
3. It is good that you *do*.

It is important to emphasize the need for mankind to reject utilitarian values, i.e., "you are good if you do something useful." No; first, a person must know and feel that he is good in and because of himself. Knowing and feeling affirmed, then like Anna Dengel, a person can *do* much without sacrificing his own dignity or the dignity of others. *Doing* for the affirmed person is emotionally fulfilling because it is now in proper perspective.

Adventure

Adventure is an aspect of the life of the affirmed person. Living with a sense of spontaneity and ambition, one sees and brings the goodness out in other persons and things. Affirmed persons can find happiness in their work, family life, and even in the midst of some suffering and lack of material goods, because they know and feel that they are basically "loveable" persons. Excessive workloads are not allowed; but hard work is not avoided. Time, for the affirmed person, allows for leisure, work, play and prayer.

Ambition

Christian theology has warned us a great deal about the dangers of pride and excessive ambition. There are writers on love, throughout the centuries, who have commented that excessive ambition leads to a path of inevitable self-destruction.

However, little has been said about the opposite side — refusing to be what you can be. Ambition and affirmation need not be at opposite poles. The affirmed person will take delight in becoming everything he can be without overly *striving* in a functionalistic manner.

Jaroslav Pelikan

The Lutheran theologian, Jaroslav Pelikan, in his thought provoking essay, *Toward a Theology of Ambition*, writes: "The Christian declaration that Jesus of Nazareth is the Christ, the Son of God and Savior of the world, makes it possible for us to take the risks demanded in a life of ambition. We can afford to lose only because we know that, on account of his crucifixion and resurrection, we ultimately cannot lose . . . The moral corollary of the theological doctrine of creation is not only Christian humility, but also Christian ambition, the acceptance of the possibilities that God has placed before us and into us and the resolution that these possibilities shall not be allowed to lie fallow. It is not piety, but blasphemy, to neglect them on the supposition that the glory of God is magnified when the potential of man is belittled. The accomplishment of all that God intends for a man is not an alpha-point at the beginning, but an omega-point at the end, toward which a man accepts the gifts of God and affirms them with gratitude."

Creation

I believe that Anna Dengel and all affirmed people live what Pelikan and others theorize concerning the "virtue of Christian ambition." The affirmed person understands that he is not just an object of God's affirmation; but that he actually participates in the continued creativity with our world. The affirmed person realizes that he has (and the significant other helps him to develop) a potential within himself which should be realized.

Love of Oneself

Doctor Pelikan goes on in his essay to develop another term for Christian ambition, namely, "sanctified love of oneself." He borrows the brilliant insight of St. Bernard of Clairvaux who teaches about the nature of love. St. Bernard states that the highest form of love is "to learn to love myself for God's sake." Denial, always knocking myself down, belittling my talents, would be akin to denying that God's beauty is within me. The Lord, in the parables, reminded us that His Father desires that we develop and share whatever gifts we have to further his Kingdom and to add to our own happiness in this life and the next.

Creative Assertion

Authentically ambitious persons will be moved to be creatively *assertive*. They will know that they cannot always be controlled by the fear of hurting other people's feelings. One does not affirm while denying one's own individuality, territory, or principles. Thomas More, lawyer, family man, and saint, is an outstanding example of an affirmer who is an assertive person. Robert Bolt, in his play, *A Man For All Seasons*, places these words on the lips of Thomas More, the former Lord Chancellor of England, just before he was put to death:

> If we lived in a world where virtue was profitable, common sense would make us good, and greed would make us saintly. And we would live like angels in the happy land that needs no heroes. But since in fact we see that avarice, anger, envy, pride, sloth, lust and stupidity commonly profit far beyond humility, chastity, fortitude, justice and thought, and have to choose to be human at all . . . why then perhaps we MUST stand fast, . . . even at the risk of being heroes.[23]

Summary

Thus, we have briefly reflected on the relationship of affirmation to ambition. We can see that the affirmed person can *do* much, once he properly accepts the love of others, feels he is loveable, and understands the sanctifying power of grace with its contribution to the continued affirmation so necessary in a technological age. Spontaneity and joy are the products of affirmation which make ambition an adventure — without which, ambition would be a tyrant.

chapter eight

FEELING AND DOING
IN GROUP LIVING

O Jesus, help me to become human.
— Teilhard De Chardin

Have you ever listened to a song and said, "Ah, those lyrics capture just what I am feeling now!"? I believe that all good music has in common a plaintive quality that makes us feel, "Ah, there's a person who understands me; that person knows how I feel . . ."

Affirmation and Feelings

We have stated that the affirmed person is aware of his or her felt lovableness and goodness; it is not just a matter of knowing. It is important to stress that *all feelings are good.* Yes, all feelings are good! They are not indifferent or bad in themselves. God created our feelings to help us live richly and fully.

All feelings tell us something about ourselves. Joy tells us something; but so does anger. It is *reason* that must inform and help govern our feelings. But, at first, we must be comfortable about being "feeling persons" and not be frightened or thrown into panic because of what is primary and most natural to mankind: that the human person has feelings. Once we declare all our feelings are good and become emotionally comfortable with this human reality, we have the opportunity to grow in affirmation and be affirmed and affirming individuals.

Comfortable and Uncomfortable Feelings

Once known and allowed to be, feelings can help us to keep life situations in proportion and help us to grow emotionally. Some feelings are comfortable, e.g. joy, trust, happiness, etc; and some may be uncomfortable, e.g. anger, hate, sadness, etc. But regardless of whether they are comfortable or uncomfortable, feelings contribute to our personalities when governed by reason. It is important that we not ignore or repress our feelings. If we try to live a life escaping from our feelings or trying to live as if they have nothing to do with our personalities, then we are putting ourselves in a dangerous position. It is so important that the young be properly educated in regard to a good understanding of the role feelings and emotions play in their lives, so they do not grow into adulthood trying to ignore feelings or to live in a state of guilt about something so ordinarily beautiful and so nobly creative.

Repression and Suppression

It is important not only to develop healthy expression of feelings, but to understand the difference between repression and suppression of feelings. "Repression," a term introduced by Freud, is an *unconscious* defense mechanism in which a person removes from consciousness those ideas, impulses, and effects that are unacceptable to the person. "Suppression" is a *conscious* act of controlling and inhibiting an unacceptable impulse, emotion, or idea. Suppression is differentiated from repression in that the latter is an unconscious process. All must, at times, effect suppression in regard to feelings if we are to have a healthy mental life. However, repression often leads to emotional illness.

Feelings and Spiritual Life

My Jesuit colleague, Father Bernard J. Bush, writes, "I do not think it is an exaggeration to say that until recently spirituality was largely a matter of God up there and me down here. Our salvation was worked out by following the precepts of the Church, the rules of our religious communities, confessing our sins regularly, receiving the Eucharist, and adhering to established devotional practices. We were convinced that if we did these things faithfully we would become holy and save our souls. Community life was devoted to what we used to call edification, a kind of competition for holiness which reduced itself largely to external observance. What we may have been feeling internally was of little interest; attention was directed to development of the will. There was little attempt to work at a happy marriage of faith and feeling. In fact, feelings were considered a positive detriment to sanctity. I remember a popular sarcastic adage about Jesuits which we used to repeat with some pride, 'They meet without affection, live in silence, and part without regret.' Since the intellectual powers of memory, intellect, and will were considered to be the highest and most noble parts of the soul, we spent years cultivating them. The effect of such training on the emotional lives of many of us was devastating. Somehow what was going on deep inside in the form of anger, love, depression, joy, sorrow, yearning, longing, loneliness, and so forth, did not seem to have much connection to the faith life. In the context of this kind of spiritual bookkeeping, there was an almost constant preoccupation with the state of our souls, adding up the credits and debits with categories such as mortal sin, venial sin and faults against nature. Even after we counted up the balance sheet in an examination of conscience, we were never quite sure what God really thought about us and we would go to confession just to make sure. So the question naturally arises, just what does God think or feel about me? The stage is now set for a form of idolatry.

Projection

"Because we are time and earth bound we have a hard time accepting an image of God that is really like God. That is, we tend to make God into our image and likeness. When the question about God's feelings for me arises, the most convenient base for measurement is my own feelings about myself. One of the ordinary mechanisms of defense against anxiety is projection. Projection is attributing to someone else the welcome or unwelcome thoughts and feelings that I have myself. If I am troubled by what I consider to be immoral thoughts, I will tend to attribute immoral motives to the actions of others. I say to myself, 'I know what would be on my mind if I were doing that, so it must be on their mind too.' I believe that much false religion is projection. The gods of the pagans were largely the projections of the seven deadly sins of humanity. Those gods demanded propitiation for wrongs perpetrated against them. They were capricious, fickle, and unpredictable. The effort to placate them required elaborate expiatory rituals to somehow win their favor or at least buy time from the wrath and fury of these stern, jealous, unloving, relentless gods. Now no one that I know would use these words to describe the God of Abraham, Isaac, Jacob, Jesus, and you and me. Yet do we not often in practice act as if he were like the pagan gods?

"These feelings come from within ourselves and are projected outward into the mind of God. We may find that we must punish ourselves mercilessly for real or imagined sins, and even then we will not forgive ourselves. I have seen people who feel as if they are the possessors of the unforgivable sin. Consequently we hold out on our acceptance of other persons until they meet our criteria for acceptable attitudes, dress, mannerisms, actions. It is good to have strong hate for evil actions. Yet have we not all found ourselves at times going beyond this to hate the sinner as well, and feeling quite righteous since we believed that God felt the same way? This is projection. It is the effect of original sin and we all have it. Fortunately, Christ has revealed the real God to us in unmistakably human form, exposed projection for the idolatry that it is, and given us the way to become free from it. It takes a profound conversion to accept the belief that God is tender and loves us just as we are, not in spite of our sins and faults, but with them.

"God does not condone or sanction evil, but he does not withhold his love because there is evil in us. The key to this understanding is found in the way we feel about ourselves. We cannot even stand or accept love from another human being when we do not love ourselves, much less believe or accept that God could possibly love us."[24]

In the light of what Father Bush teaches us concerning feelings and the spiritual life, it is good to take note of Dr. Adrian Van Kaam's words, "The feelings I refuse to own and work through in God's light may be twofold. They may be sexual, proud, arrogant, possessive, envious, jealous — briefly, they can be any feelings whose very existence in me I feel to be incompatible with my illusion of righteousness. We are interested especially in looking at feelings of anger and aggression denied in myself because of a contrived gentility. Anger and aggression perverted for this reason are a major source of pietistic anxiety."[25]

In our consideration, I would like to reflect on the two feelings that I find most threatening to those persons suffering from a lack of affirmation. There of course are others; some of which have been treated elsewhere in this book.

Anger

We must allow ourselves to feel anger while using reason to govern this feeling. It is inevitable in life's situations that when a group of people come together conflict and anger will arise. There are creative ways of expressing and accepting feelings of anger.

We mistrust anger often because little education was given to us as children that we can be very angry without being dangerous. When we repress anger, we inevitably pay some price for this denial of our true selves. Physical illness and clinical depression are often the results of turning anger in on one's self.

Anger's value as a healthy feeling can be creative when it means less punishment of ourselves and helps develop more honest and effective relationships with others. Feelings of anger can be expressed in a family or any group if we learn that anger is only one aspect of reality and need not be a threat. The family or group can help us to express our anger and can also help us to assess our expression of anger. Anger cannot be allowed to be used as a tool to manipulate another person or a group.

Often the *significant other* may have to accept the anger of the one who is being affirmed. But remember, this acceptance is not unconditional; there is always room for the *significant other* to be supportively confrontal. Speaking on the creative uses of anger, Marshall Bryant Hodge writes: "Sometimes when we feel angry we will suspect our anger is based on a misinterpretation. And yet it still bothers us. The best approach, as in other situations, is to express all our feelings, not just the anger. Thus we might say something like this: 'I may be reading you completely wrong, but that comment you made as you were leaving this morning has really been bugging me.'

"To be able to recognize, and let others know that we recognize, that we are prone (like everyone else) to misunderstanding others will often open the door to more creative resolutions of anger. Very often, of course, misinterpretations have occurred on both sides and a thorough airing of feeljngs will lead to a new understanding and new awareness of love. . . .

"Such an attitude involves a feeling of self-worth in which one *feels* lovable and assumes the other person cares. The feeling, 'He's angry with me, so he must not love me,' does not enter the picture. The individual is also sufficiently unafraid to love that he can enjoy the encounter of love even in its angry form. He also does not condemn himself for being angry."[26]

This brief reflection on the feeling of anger does not mean to suggest that all anger must be expressed at all times. Suppression, as previously noted, involves free choice. There may be situations when we would choose to suppress anger and we do so with full awareness that such behavior would bring about a greater good. If it is suppression of anger, and not fear of anger, then we are not on a pattern of self-destruction. But even in this situation, it would be advisable to discuss the anger with an independent third party or some friend outside the situation.

Loneliness

It is important to note that all persons must learn to accept a certain sense of loneliness. This is true even for those who live in groups, married or single persons. "You mean *aloneness*," may be your first reaction. No, I mean that all persons must come to understand that from time to time we will suffer a gut level feeling of loneliness. Loneliness is an acute feeling of twentieth century mankind amidst his technology and "age of space." For me, loneliness is a demonstration of original sin which has left us all emotionally imperfect.

Excessive loneliness is a predominant feeling of the non-affirmed person. As the significant other becomes more important in an individual's life, excessive loneliness dissipates while the individual's awareness of his dignity is increased.

Once we acknowledge the rough edges of loneliness, we can develop this feeling which leads to creativity and not depression or anxiety. When we are apart from a group, we can gain insight into our own individuality. It is out of the experience of loneliness and separation, and the consequent experience of reunion and belonging, that further individualization and healing occurs.

"To kill time" is a horrible cliché and devastating way to live. We can develop a sense of creative loneliness. We can enjoy spending time being gentle to ourselves by being present to ourselves and doing things we like. In his meditation, *Out of Solitude,* Henri J. M. Nouwen reminds us: "To live a Christian life means to live *in* the world without being of it. It is in solitude that this inner freedom can grow. Jesus went to a lonely place to pray, that is, to grow in the awareness that all the power he had was given to him; that all the words he spoke came from his Father; and that all the works he did were not really his but the works of the One who had sent him. In the lonely place Jesus was made free to fail.

"A life without a lonely place, that is, a life without a quiet corner, easily becomes destructive. When we cling to the results of our actions as our only way to self-identification, then we become possessive and defensive and tend to look at our fellow human beings more as enemies to be kept at a distance than as friends with whom we share the gifts of life."[27]

Doing

When we grow in comfort regarding ourselves as being "feeling" human persons, activity takes on new meaning. Activity itself does not become a means for escaping myself and my feelings but offers an emotional experience of the richness that comes from our feelings. Before any "doing" can be emotionally fruitful, it must be preceded by the feelings of relaxation, inner calm and solitude. Otherwise, the "world of work" will try to claim the whole field of human existence.

We have already spoken briefly (in chapter seven) of *The Adventure of Ambitious Affirmation,* and pointed to the fact that the affirmed person can *do* much because he feels loved much, knows the value of leisure, and enjoys work and the emotional satisfaction coming from a day's labor. Work which is preceded by rest is always a *doing* that is constructive and a proper living out of the corporal and spiritual works of mercy. Such work yields much emotional satisfaction. Such work does not mean that I *become* my work; such work does not mean a further denial of my loveableness; but such work affirms, gives strength to, and makes strong my concept of myself and my neighbor. "Workaholism" is not the way of life for the affirmed person.

Christ invites his followers to be feelers of their feeling, doers of their work, thinkers of thoughts, when He says: "Think of the wild flowers, and how they neither work nor weave. Yet I tell you that Solomon in all his glory was never arrayed like one of these. If God so clothes the grass, which flowers in the field today and is burned in the stove tomorrow, is he not much more likely to clothe you, you of little faith? You must not set your heart on what you eat or drink, nor must you live in a state of anxiety. The whole heathen world is busy about getting food and drink, and your Father knows well enough that you need such things. No, set your heart on his kingdom, and your food and drink will come as a matter of course." (Matt 6: 28-34)

Responsibility

Note that the emphasis in affirmation is primarily with *being* and not *doing*. Such is essential to an understanding of the psychotheology of affirmation. Caution is needed, however, so that we not lose perspective.

Affirmation is not part of a falsely idealistic and unreal world where we all live, where there is no responsibility or productivity. No, such a view would be contrary to a proper understanding of affirmation. The emphasis on a balanced view of being and feeling is in reaction to utilitarianism and functionalism. The affirmed person can work hard, be active *and* restful, and enjoy affective and effective relationship with the world because of the harmony he knows in his own life. He can be the free dancer, enhanced with new life, new meaning and new successes. When one's life is affirmed, any occasion is an opportunity for singing aloud the joy of being alive! The affirmed person desires and is not afraid . . .

> *To stand tall in the sunlight*
> > *To seek out the bright face of beauty.*
> > *To reach for the dream, the star.*
> *To see the world through eyes of tenderness.*
> > *To love with open heartedness.*
> *To speak the quiet word of comforting.*
> *To look up the mountain*
> > *and not be afraid to climb.*
> *To be aware of the needs of others.*
> *To believe in the wonder of life,*
> > *the miracle of creation,*
> > *the rapture of love,*
> > *the beauty of the universe,*
> > *the dignity of the human being.*[28]

chapter nine

AN AFFIRMATION COMMUNITY: A PSYCHOTHEOLOGICAL MODEL

Everyone has inside himself
A piece of good news!
The good news is that you really don't know
how great you can be
how much you can love
what you can accomplish and
what your potential is.
How can you top good news like that?
                              —The Diary of Anne Frank

The "good news" at the House of Affirmation, the International Therapeutic Center for Clergy and Religious in Whitinsville, Massachusetts, is at the service of all priests and religious who are not embarrassed to become more fulfilled and healthier persons. The House of Affirmation is dedicated to the positive concept that we have "good news" within us that we really do not know as yet. This "good news" will emerge when we have become affirmed persons. The non-affirmed personality expresses itself in those problems of neurosis examined in chapter four: emotional and mental discomfort, alcoholism and addiction, erratic homosexuality, compulsive heterosexual behavior, and other symptoms of unhappiness and confusion.

The primary service of the House of Affirmation is to treat, care for, and cure clergy and religious who have non-affirmed identities, and therefore feel ineffective or unhappy. The apostolate of the House of Affirmation is of crucial importance, not only to priests and religious whom we serve, but to the entire Church. John Cardinal Wright, Prefect for the Clergy in the Vatican, has said recently: "The need of the House of Affirmation is beyond any doubt considerable and urgent."

The apostolate has already served many priests and religious throughout the world and its full residential program, founded in 1973, has already assisted priests and religious from seven continents.

It may sound trite, but what the House of Affirmation is all about is a blend of love and science, offering vocational and emotional guidance to priests and religious in the hour of need, "the dark night of the soul and mind."

A Beginning

The House of Affirmation is a direct outgrowth, broadened in scope, of the Consulting Center for Clergy and Religious of the Diocese of Worcester, established a few years ago as the result of a request by the Senate of Religious to Auxiliary Bishop Timothy J. Harrington.

In 1970 Bishop Bernard J. Flanagan initiated the proposed center under the directorship of Sister Anna Polcino, S.C.M.M., M.D., a practicing psychiatrist. In the early stages, I joined Sister Anna as a priest-psychotherapist. The project expanded from a local diocesan effort to a nationwide service to clergy and religious with emotional problems.

The overriding goal of the early out-patient clinic, known as the Consulting Center, was to help priests and religious to become fully human, consistently free persons within the context of their ecclesial calling and society. Sister Anna and I tried to meet this goal through a three-fold program of service, education and research. Since its opening, the services and programs of the House of Affirmation have included individual consultation, group consultation, group process communication labs, personal growth groups, candidate assessment, lectures and workshops.

After two full years of operation as a non-residential Center, it became apparent to Dr. Anna, myself, and significant others, that the out-patient facilities were not sufficient. There was a definite need for an intensive residential treatment program. Thus the House of Affirmation Residential Center was conceived. The Residential Center became a reality in Whitinsville, October 1973, when the doors opened to welcome its first residents. This was the genesis of today's House of Affirmation.

Residential Center

Results were startlingly rapid. Having been incorporated by the State of Massachusetts, we set about securing a site for the work. Here the Lasell Ecumenical Retreat House, owned by the Episcopal Diocese of Western Massachusetts, came into the picture.

Bishop Alexander D. Stewart, the Episcopal bishop, encouraged us by offering the Whitinsville estate with eleven acres and three main buildings including the mansion built in 1896. The main building was donated by the Episcopal bishop to our work for one dollar. However, to assure our privacy and obtain another eleven-year-old building on the property, which was necessary to house priests and religious who came to us, a minimal cost of purchase was set at $55,000. This amount was granted by the DeRance Foundation of Milwaukee, Wisconsin.

Now that we had a roof over our heads, much work was needed. Where would be the chapel? Try the billiard room! What about the lecture hall? Perhaps the music room! Breakfast room? Perhaps the storage room off the kitchen! Doctors' offices? The master bedroom, the next two principal bedrooms! What about furniture? Check the attic, the former stables, the cellar! Painting, papering, cleaning, sanding, and other work remained. So, those who came to us in the early days could scrounge; and we did our best with the assistance of many Brothers who were jacks-of-all-trades. Thus the House of Affirmation took physical shape.

The first resident was Father Bill who had left his teaching community years before, to hide his unhappiness under the glitter and paint of a traveling circus — "LADIES AND GENTLEMEN, THE G-R-E-A-T-E-S-T S-H-O-W O-N E-A-R-T-H."

Still, amidst his running away, the priesthood remained of value in Father Bill's heart and soul. But his Order, when he applied for reinstatement, told him he needed to be evaluated. Within two months, Father Bill, after receiving treatment at the House of Affirmation, was back where he had really wanted to be — within his religious community, exercising his priesthood, teaching in the classroom, offering youngsters and others the wisdom of the ages as weighed by his personal experiences. A dramatic evolution of the vocation of a man called to God!

Professional Staff

Clearly, the building is not what "House of Affirmation" means. The House of Affirmation is *people*, those who staff it as well as residents who come to it. So, at this point, I wish to introduce in particular our founder, Sister Anna Polcino, S.C.M.M., M.D., senior psychiatrist with the State of Massachusetts Department of Mental Health. A graduate of Women's Medical College of Pennsylvania, in that state, for nine years she was a missionary surgeon in West Pakistan and Bangladesh. She did her psychiatric residency at Worcester State Hospital; is presently staff member of St. Vincent Hospital and Worcester State Hospital; and is instructor in psychiatry at the University of Massachusetts Medical School. In 1965 she was given an award as an Outstanding Missionary. She is presently psychiatric director of therapy at the House of Affirmation and president of the diocesan Senate of Religious. Recently she became the first woman, and nun, ever elected to the Presidency of the National Guild of Catholic Psychiatrists.

Other professionals joined us in the early days: priest-psychologists, sister-psychologists, lay-psychologists, psychiatrists, nurses, all willing to take the risk of dedicating their lives to the restoration of priests and religious to happy ministry. A picture of the whole Church emerged from the staff made up of diocesan priests, religious priests, brothers, nuns, and lay persons, married and single. According to our accreditations, the leadership of the House of Affirmation is academically excellent and fully experienced.

Program

But what do we actually do?

First, the House of Affirmation is a place for people

who wish to reassess their vocational and spiritual life in the light of their emotional problems. The House of Affirmation is not a mental institution; it is a center for priests and religious where psycho-spiritual problems may be handled in a therapeutic residential community of men and women while they are experiencing individual counseling and group therapy.

It is not a nesting place for those unfit for ministry. Residents are accepted only after thorough evaluation. They are made aware that the day they arrive at the House of Affirmation they are being prepared to leave it. Residents are really on an open campus. They may use their cars, if they have them, and are free to go and come, keeping in mind the internal schedule of the house.

At the House of Affirmation, priests and religious have an opportunity to re-affirm their religious identity so they can live happy, useful lives within the communal structures of their religious communities or diocesan discipline. During a visit to the House of Affirmation, Cardinal Alfrink commented: "Very often the world of today experiences the religious person as one who is not happy himself and does not make others happy. . . . This is not the intention of the Lord's message and of our being Christians. The message of the Lord is a message of salvation — happy tidings — a message of love and joy."

The laity should not be surprised to find that there is need for a center such as the House of Affirmation. In many ways, a priest or religious is no different from someone in another segment of society. Immaturity and the pressures of the twentieth century exert great forces upon many people before their entrance to seminary or religious life, causing deprivation results to show up later in life.

Philosophy of the House of Affirmation

The philosophy underlying the House of Affirmation's existence and operation can be succinctly stated as: treatment of the whole person in a wholly therapeutic environment. Priests and religious who come to us are accepted for who they are as people. While offering them what we feel is some of the best psychiatric and psychological knowledge and therapy, the professional staff, at the same time, shares the Christian value system and encourages the priests and religious in their vocational choice and identity.

Priests and religious have chosen a celibate way of life which jars with the usual Freudian model of therapy. An alternative had to evolve to meet the needs of this relatively important and clearly delineated sociological group of celibate religious professionals seeking psychological help.

Modern psychology emphasizes the tremendous power of the environment on human development and behavior; our surroundings exert a molding influence on our behavior. In milieu therapy, the expectancies and attitudes of the treatment staff are central to bringing about social rehabilitation.

The House of Affirmation provides a favorable environment for the social re-learning that constitutes therapy. But the psychotheological community concept of the House of Affirmation goes beyond milieu therapy, with its inherent psycho-analytical orientation and reductionism. Here, there is an existential concern with rediscovering the living person amid the compartmentalization and dehumanization of modern culture. Interest centers on reality as immediately experienced by the person, with accent on the inter-personal experience of the priest or religious. The House of Affirmation therapeutic community supplies the type of accepting, or impartial reactions from others, that favors social learning. Besides, the therapeutic environment prevents further disorganization in the residents' behavior by reducing their intense anxieties.

Psychotheological Therapeutic Community

The House of Affirmation has developed a unique model in its phychotheological therapeutic community. The expression "psychotheological community" implies a quest for communion with God and with man. It is an accepted fact that personhood can only be realized in community, and this phenomenological aspect of man's human predicament aligns the model with the existential therapeutic movement. It seeks to analyze the structure of the person's human existence in view of understanding the reality underlying his *being-in-crisis*. It is concerned with the profound dimensions of contemporary emotional and spiritual temper. The need of a psychotheological community looms large in the current psychological literature.

When they come to the House of Affirmation, each priest and religious in the community remains a unique individual. He may grow and change in the community; but he will retain his identity, or grow in awareness of what his true identity as a Christian person is. Unity and charity, openness, receptivity, sharing, giving and receiving, are some of the favorable conditions present at the House of Affirmation, among staff and residents, that allow the troubled priest or religious to re-assess his whole vocational commitment. Bernard Haring, C.Ss.R., the distinguished moral theologian, has made the following observation of the House of Affirmation: "I think the House of Affirmation is an excellent opportunity for bringing peace to the heart and the mind of people who are meant to be peacemakers."

The post-Vatican II period demands maturity and balance on the part of those chosen to minister to the people of God because much risk is involved. Many priests and religious, since Vatican II, have floundered in the slow and painful assimilation of change. Confusion, doubt and a sense of loss have taxed the coping ability of many priests and religious who, cut off from safe moorings, question their identity and authenticity in what they consider an uncharted land.

Based on St. Thomas Aquinas

In its psychotheological approach, the House of Affirmation is based on the rich anthropology of St. Thomas Aquinas, and the best of modern clinical psychiatry, in complete unity with the magisterium and tradition of the Roman Catholic Church. For this reason, it exists to be of service to priests and religious. Humberto Cardinal Medeiros, Archbishop of Boston, has recently stated: "Already the good work of the House of Affirmation is known, not only nationally but internationally. The excellent treatment given to priests and religious has benefited in incalculable ways the mission of Holy Mother Church."

As stated previously, the House of Affirmation is neither a place of confinement, nor a haven for rest and recreation; rather, it is a miniature social-religious community planned and controlled for facilitating the social learning of its residents. The professional staff members have accepted as the general goal of psychotherapy: to help the "unfree", childishly dependent person become a genuine adult capable of responding affirmatively to life, people and society. The focus is on self-understanding and insight-building, of an immediate and current nature, with a view toward helping the priest and religious grasp the meaning of his existence in its historical totality. Ultimately, the mentally healthy priest and religious will attain freedom to choose maturity in outlook and responsible independence.

Appreciation of the Healthy Celibate

The life of the celibate priest or religious can be viewed as an ongoing process of interaction with the religious, social, and natural forces that make up the environment. The meaning that life assumes for a celibate depends on the person's response to these forces. The celibate community constitutes a union of persons who participate in a common love-response to the call of Christ. The key to a proper understanding of community life lies in *participation* which becomes a unifying force while allowing for individual differences. Is not willingness to receive from another one of the dearest gifts one can give to the other? Participation characterizes the relationship of individuals united by love in community. All encounters assume meaning in that context; they become avenues of development.

The difference one's presence makes in the overall community process gives meaning to the celibate's life. Being human really means coming to grips, in a creative way, with the concrete situation in which we find ourselves. The here-and-now experience is crucial, for life is today— not yesterday, or tomorrow.

The same applies in the therapeutic situation, be it individual or group; the ongoing, immediate experience of residents and therapists, as they interact, becomes the phenomenological emphasis in psychotherapy. The total phenomena experienced at any moment in time makes up man's existential situation; the experienced event is what is brought to therapy. Listening to another as person, looking into his eyes, mind and heart with deep sympathy, feeling that this person is suffering — is appealing to us as persons. Are these not affirmative responses to Christ's summons: "Love one another as I have loved you."? (Jn 13:34-35)

The call to Christian life is ideally expressed in the experience of the Eucharist, the community experience par excellence. The Eucharist builds up a *community of faith* and so stands at the very center of the psychotheological community of the House of Affirmation. It reveals the solidarity of all members in Christ. It is the same solidarity that is expressed in the opening words of the *Pastoral Constitution on the Church in the Modern World*: "The joys and hopes, the sorrows and worries of men of our time are ours." (Gs. Art. 1)

Challenge of Vatican II

The House of Affirmation has thus accepted the challenge of the Fathers of Vatican II who urged us, in their *Pastoral Constitution on the Church in the Modern World*, to make appropriate use "not only of the theological principles, but also of the findings of the secular sciences, especially of psychology and sociology" (Gs. Art. 62) to help the faithful live their faith in a more thorough and mature way.

In its *Decree on the Appropriate Renewal of the Religious Life*, the Council Fathers pursued the same line of thought: "The matter of living, praying, and working should be suitably adapted to the physical and psychological conditions of today's religious . . . to the needs of the apostolate, the requirements of a given culture, the social and economic circumstances." (PC, Art. 3)   In the article pertaining to chastity, religious are urged to "take advantage of those natural helps which favor mental and bodily health . . . Everyone should remember that chastity has stronger safeguards in a community when true fraternal love thrives among its members." (PC, Art. 12)

It is believed that celibate, religious professionals trained in psychiatry and psychology can bring their own experience to bear in coming to a better understanding of the emotional problems of the religious and priestly life of today. Such is the case in the two satellite offices and in the Residential Treatment Center of the House of Affirmation.

For too long, celibates have been stigmatized when seeking professional help from psychiatrists and psychologists who had little understanding of their religious commitment; the misconceptions often deterred religious and priests from seeking psychiatric-psychological help. The residential treatment center has been designed to minimize the threat and possible alienation attendant on presenting oneself to a professional establishment. A homelike atmosphere has been developed which has proved most therapeutic and which prepares the priest and religious to respond to therapy in a very positive manner in contrast to the resistance usually found when working with the laity.

All Must Enter Willingly

An individual priest, sister or brother may be referred to the House of Affirmation for the purpose of coming to a better understanding of his emotional problems and/or resolving them. However, the priest or religious is always informed that unless he comes of his own free will, therapy will be of little avail to him. No resident is accepted for treatment on the mere recommendation of his religious superiors; the priest or religious must indicate willingness to come for therapy.

The principle of *confidentiality* is crucial to the operation of the House of Affirmation; privacy is maintained at all times. This has produced a sense of security and trust, and the number of priests and religious residents has grown geometrically.

Since its inception, it has been stressed that the purpose of the House of Affirmation Centers is not so much to keep the celibate in the religious or priestly life as to help him become truly human and consistently free. Through therapy, the priest or religious can come to his own decision about his future.

In the course of therapy, the priest or religious comes to view his experience in greater perspective and regains a future orientation. Self-growth demands that the person have something to aim for, a goal which can be brought into reality through committed action. The task of the priest or religious will then be to actualize the possibility and make it a reality. As a person begins to respond to his feelings, he sees possibilities in his future, makes attemps to achieve them, and his life-style becomes increasingly independent.

Contrary to the opinions of some, it is our scientific finding that celibacy is not the prime problem of people who are in vocational crisis or have emotional disturbance. As a matter of fact, many times the vocational crisis itself is a reflection, not so much of dissatisfaction with the Church, or the priesthood, or religious life, but with underlying emotional immaturity resulting from a lack of affirmation.

Many of the problems encountered at the House of Affirmation may be classified as deprivation syndromes, and what Freud has described as the repressive neurosis. In the first case, lack of love and acceptance (lack of affirmation) has crippled the psychological functioning of the priest or religious; in the latter case, one encounters a priest or religious who has made excessive use of the defense mechanism known as *intellectualization*. The individuals are not aware of their emotions and have even repressed anger in their lives as celibates. The repression came about by faulty training which presented the emotion of anger as "unvirtuous," an emotion not to be expressed at any time. Yet, Christ found it appropriate to express his emotions: "the angry Man who picked up a cord to drive the buyers and sellers out of the temple, Who wept in sadness over Jerusalem, Who was bathed in sweat before His arrest," was not a stoical, emotionless Man.

Through therapy, individual priests and religious become aware of their emotions, are informed that their emotions are basically good, and are encouraged to express them in a healthy way within the context of a celibate life. Individual therapy is supported by group therapy where angry feelings may be expressed and accepted as such. The re-educative process is somewhat long and painful but pays off in a more personally satisfying and productive life.

Self-Supporting Apostolate

The work of the House of Affirmation is completely self-supporting. It receives no allotted funds from any diocese or religious community. The House of Affirmation is entirely dependent for its material functioning on donations from interested foundations, concerned members of the laity, and gifts from some of the residents who come to us.

Since the House of Affirmation is a faith community deeply rooted in the teaching of the Gospel, we believe that the Lord will provide for its day-to-day material needs. Our own Bishop and member of the Board of Directors, Bernard J. Flanagan, has written: "I am convinced that there is a growing need and demand for the kind of therapy which the House of Affirmation, with a professionally competent staff, is able to offer priests and religious. I am confident that it is in good hands, and join with all of you in prayer that it will merit the wide support which it deserves."

The Chapel of the Holy Spirit at the House of Affirmation is symbolic of the spiritual principles of its therapeutic and educational programs which are available to priests and religious with emotional and spiritual problems. The Eucharist is the center of daily life at the House of Affirmation; and it is here that we entrust our spiritual, emotional and intellectual needs to the Lord.

Patron: St. Therese of Lisieux

In a special way St. Therese of Lisieux is very close to the House of Affirmation. Adopted as the patron of the House of Affirmation, St. Therese's example of affectionate, unselfish love of others serves as a model of the well-spring of new life for lonely and non-affirmed priests and religious. Therese's doctrine, perfected in a life-span of only twenty-four years, has been called by His Holiness Pope Paul VI one of the truly life-giving religious currents of our day. It constitutes an intimate part of the philosophy of the House of Affirmation.

The Ripple Effect

To adequately grasp the spirit and gifts of the House of Affirmation requires a visit, to see the hope, the joy of the priests and religious, and the dedicated zeal of staff—from the qualified psychiatric and psychological personnel to the housekeeping and kitchen workers. From the House of Affirmation, priests and religious who have been affirmed by the staff and healed of their spiritual and/or emotional problems (or at least worked toward their resolution), leave us and become renewed and refreshed, as they once again serve the Church and society. One priest returned to the parish, or one religious returned to the classroom or other apostolate, has significant influence upon many people. Thus, we believe the ripple effect of the House of Affirmation is most significant.

Summary

One priest recently told me that the feeling he had upon leaving the happy House of Affirmation is reflected in the last two lines of Emma Lazarus' poem, "The New Colossus," inscribed on the Statue of Liberty:

Send these, the homeless, tempest-tos't, to me—
I lift my lamp beside the golden door.

The House of Affirmation is indeed *a lamp* to those in the "dark night of the soul"; and the *golden door* for them is the door that opens back out to the world of religious affirmation and *identity-aware* service of God and man.

Jesus relies on His clergy and religious. He has made a big investment in them. They "re-present" His Spirit and message; but only a healthy and affirmed personality can do justice to this responsibility. The House of Affirmation goes beyond the purely psychological analysis in its particular sensitivity to the religious dimension of the personality. Many priests and religious who leave the House of Affirmation return to active ministry and, for the first time, joyfully realize the words of Christ: "My yoke is easy, and My burden light."

chapter ten

AFFIRMATION REFLECTIONS

The following reflections have been gathered over a long period of time by my clients and students who have found them wise reflections meaningful to their growth in affirmation. Many words are written thousands of times; but to make them truly our own, we must honestly reflect on them over and over again. Then, at some spontaneous moment, they will find meaning in our personal experience. Indeed, these words can be healing touches of affirmation.

Each child is a new being
a potential prophet
a new spiritual prince,
a new spark of life precipitated into the outer darkness.
Who are we to decide that it is hopeless?

— R. D. Laing

Every person must have a concern for self,
and feel a responsibility to discover his mission in life.
God has given each normal person a capacity to achieve
    some end.
True, some are endowed with more talent than others,
but God has left none of us talentless.

Potential powers of creativity are within us,
and we have the duty to work assiduously
to discover these powers.

— Martin Luther King

No man knows how much he is an optimist, even when
he calls himself a pessimist, because he has not already
measured the depths of his debt to whatever created him
and enabled him to call himself anything. At the back of
our brains, so to speak, there was a forgotten blaze or
burst of astonishment at our own existence.

— G. K. Chesterton

To care means first of all
to empty our own cup
and to allow the other
to come close to us.

— Henri Nouwen

I feel warm and loving toward myself,
for I am a unique and precious being,
ever doing the best my current awareness permits.

— L. S. Barksdale

Love is the first gift.
Whatever else is freely given to us
becomes a gift only through love.

— Thomas Aquinas

The capacity to grasp values,
to affirm them,
and to respond to them,
is the foundation for realizing moral values of man.

— Dietrich Von Hildebrand

By affirming our being
we participate in the self-affirmation
of being-itself.
There are no valid arguments
for the "existence" of God,
but there are acts of courage
in which we affirm the power of being,
whether we know it or not.
If we know it, we accept acceptance consciously.
If we do not know it,
we nevertheless accept it and participate in it.
And in our acceptance of that
which we do not know
the power of being is manifest to us.
Courage has revealing power,
the courage to be is the key
to being-itself.   — Paul Tillich

There is no greater invitation to love
than loving first.   — St. Augustine

When I look at your heavens,
the work of your hands,
the moon and the stars which you established;
what is man
that you think of him
or the son of man
that you care for him?
Yet you made him little less than God,
and you crown him with glory and honor.
You gave him dominion
over the works of your hands;
You have put all things
under his feet.   — Psalm 8:36

That is the true season of love,
when we believe
that we alone can love,
that no one could ever have loved so
before us,
and that no one will love
in the same way after us.

—Goethe

Anyone who courageously accepts life—
even a shortsighted, primitive positivist
who apparently bears patiently
with the poverty of the superficial—
has really already accepted God.
He has accepted God as he is in himself,
as he wants to be in our regard
in love and freedom — in other words,
as the God of the eternal life
of divine self-communication
in which God himself is the center of man
and in which man's form is that of the Godman himself.
For anyone who really accepts himself,
accepts a mystery in the sense of
the infinite emptiness which is man.

— Karl Rahner

The most tragic of all,
in the long run,
is the ultimate attitude
'It doesn't matter.'

— Rollo May

Going about looking as if we were totally self-reliant
and independent and didn't need anything from anyone
is a facade hiding a deep longing for intimacy.

— Jerry Greenwald

A man who trims himself to suit everybody
will soon whittle himself away.

— Charles Schwab

Never, "for the sake of peace and quiet,"
deny your own experience or convictions.

— Dag Hammarskjold

We are all born for love;
it is the principle of existence
and its only end.

— Benjamin Disraeli

Each (being) is said to be perfect
insofar as it attains its own end,
which is the highest perfection of anything.

— Thomas Aquinas

To Fall in Love with God
        is the greatest of all romances!
To Seek Him
        is the greatest of all adventures!
To Find Him
        is the greatest human achievement!

— Raphael Simon

The concern for man and his destiny
must always be the chief interest
of all technical effort.
Never forget it among your diagrams and equations.

— Albert Einstein

. . . if a man's life of faith has reached the stage where he has completely decided for God and wants nothing save what he wills, has he then not arrived at the inmost sphere, and is there then still a difference between his state and the highest union of love? It is very difficult here to draw the line. . . .

— Edith Stein

Love does not consist of gazing at each other but in looking in the same direction.

— Antoine De Saint-Exupery

I would rather make mistakes in kindness and compassion than work miracles in unkindness and hardness.

— Mother Teresa of Calcutta

It is our responsibility to be aware when we are talking to a person who has no ears, and continue to hope that one day we will be heard.

— Jerry Greenwald

If the word "integration" means anything, this is what it means: that we, with love, shall force our brothers to see themselves as they are, to cease fleeing from reality and begin to change it.

— James Baldwin

An appeaser is one who feeds a crocodile— hoping it will eat him last.

— Winston Churchill

The supreme happiness of life
is the conviction that we are loved—
loved for ourselves;
say, rather, loved in spite of ourselves.

— Victor Hugo

I don't shrink heads,
I help expand them!   — Anna Polcino

Don't make someTHING of yourself.

— Bernard Gunther

I would say that if there is no love,
nothing is possible.
Man absolutely cannot live by himself.

— Erich Fromm

Reasonable men can differ and remain friends.

— Harold Gould

As you may guess,
I am presently possessed by the wonder and mystery of
*   freedom—*
possessed as I have never been before
by the wonder and mystery of freedom,
meditating all the time about the foolishness of God,
who knew what it meant to make me free.
Who knew that in making me free,
He could let me succeed or fail.
Who was fool enough to let me make a choice
even about salvation or damnation.
And so it seems to me,
if He put such a terrible investment
in the grace which He gave to me;
then, indeed, grace must be the most important thing
*   of life.*

— Jacqueline Grennan

I am the inferior of any man whose rights I trample underfoot.

— Horace Greeley

*There can be no deep disappointment
where there is not deep love.*

— Martin Luther King

*Think not that you can direct the course of love,
for love, if it finds you worthy,
directs your course.*

— Kahlil Gibran

*In getting the best of our secret attachments—
ones which we cannot see
because they are principles of spiritual blindness—
our own initiative is almost always useless.
We need to leave the initiative to God.*

— Thomas Merton

Your eyes are silent tongues of love.

— Cervantes

*To love for the sake of being loved is human,
but to love for the sake of loving is angelic.*

— Lamartine

*A great deal of talent is lost in the world
for want of a little courage.
Every day sends to their graves obscure men
whom timidity prevented from making a first effort;
who, if they could have been induced to begin,
would in all probability*

have gone great lengths in the career of fame.
The fact is,
that to do anything in the world worth doing
we must not stand back shivering
and thinking of the cold and danger
but jump in
and scramble through as well as we can.

— Richard Cardinal Cushing

Love is by its nature the only power of synthesis
which in its diversifying action
is capable of raising us above the personal plane.

— Teilhard De Chardin

At least talk to each other.
To communicate is the beginning
of understanding.

Advertisement/American Tel. & Tel.

To be cut off from other human beings and their love,
to be cut off from all sense of God and of his love,
to be cut off from what one believes to be one's real self
and to be lodged in the body of a ghost who has lost the
power to love;
this is loneliness.

— Hubert Van Zeller

For you that took the all in all,
the things you left were three:
A loud voice for singing,
and clear eyes to see,
And a spouting fount of life within
that never yet has dried.

— Hilaire Belloc

The good-natured person is described in one of Paul's
letters — 'envieth not — not puffed up — not easily
provoked — seeketh no evil.'
To sum it up, his nature is GOOD.

Truth is not only violated by falsehood;
it may be equally outraged by silence.

Great victories come,
not through ease
but by fighting valiantly
and meeting hardships bravely.

Nothing which is worth doing
is ever done without great sacrifice.
Every dream in its unfolding has difficult times,
times when those who work with it are discouraged,
when it seems as though
those who were committed to it
have lost the vision.

In the mystery of social love
there is found the realization of "the other"
not only as one to be loved by us,
so that we may perfect ourselves,
but also as one who can become
more perfect by loving us.
The vocation to charity is a call not only to love
but to be loved.
The man who does not care at all
whether or not he is loved
is ultimately unconcerned about the true welfare

of the other and of society.
Hence we cannot love unless we also consent to be loved
in return.

— Thomas Merton

Creative presence to a painting by a master
tells me something
not only about a peasant or a poor man's face that will
ever be.
A faithful portrayal pierces to the depths of our shared
reality;
my look brings its meaning home to me.

—Adrian Van Kaam

You have no idea what a poor opinion I have of myself—
and how little I deserve it.

— Gilbert and Sullivan

Psychotherapy unrelated to religion or metaphysics
tends to produce an anxiously fostered middle-class
tranquility,
poisoned by its triteness.

— Przywara

I am encouraged by my living awareness of universal
literature as a single great heart, beating in response to
the cares and sorrows of our world, although these are
presented and viewed differently in its every corner.

— Alexander Solzhenitsyn

Retreat is not a flight from life
but a journey to its depth.

— Adrian Van Kaam

If you come at me with your fists doubled,
I think I can promise you
that mine will double as fast as yours;
but if you come to me and say,
"Let us sit down and take counsel together,
and, if we differ from one another,
understand just what the points at issue are,"
we will presently find that we are not
so far apart after all,
that the points on which we differ are few
and the points on which we agree are many.

— Woodrow Wilson

The magnitude love achieves is measured by its
strength of giving,
perception of understanding,
faith of purpose through the passage of time.

— Walter Rinder

Man was put on this earth as scripture tells us,
not to leave things the way they were—
God created Adam and he put him in the garden to take
    care of it —
man is supposed to transform his world
so that it bears a mark of his own intelligence
and his own art and his own concern,
because only if that is there
can there be a Christian dimension to all this.
If the world is going to be Christianized
it automatically means to be humanized.

— Bernard Cooke

If you are willing to bear serenely
the trial of being displeasing to yourself,
you will be to Jesus a pleasant place of shelter.

— St. Therese of Lisieux

A friend is one
To whom one may pour out all the contents of one's heart,
Chaff and grain together
Knowing that the
Gentlest of hands
Will take and sift it
Keep what is worth keeping
And with a breath of kindness
Blow the rest away.

— Arabian Proverb

The person who loves you has picked you out of the
*   great mass*
of uncreated clay which is humanity
to make something out of,
and the poor lumpish clay which is you
wants to find out what it has been made into.
But, at the same time, you, in the act of loving somebody,
become real,
cease to be part of the continuum
of the uncreated clay
and get the breath of life in you and rise up.
So you create yourself by creating another person,
who, however, has also created you,
picked up the you-chunk-of-clay out of the mass.
So there are two you's,
the one you yourself create by loving
and the one the beloved creates
by loving you.

— Robert Penn Warren

How vast and wonderful is the horizon
which opens before us in the quest for God.
This search does not lead us into useless, abstract
    speculation,
but gives meaning, energy and scope
to the deepest and most real appreciation of our mind.

— Pope Paul VI

PRAYER FOR AFFIRMATION

Jesus, inspired by the example of St. Therese, I place all my trust in your Sacred Heart and surrender myself to Your will. Come into my life, drive away my fears, stop my restless strivings and show me new ways of pleasing You. Teach me to discern the good in others and to love them with an affectionate smile, a gentle touch, a patient ear and an affirming word. St. Therese, pray that I will become alive again with awe and appreciation of Truth and the courage to oppose evil. Remind me always that I am created for Happiness, for the joy of living in the presence of God. St. Therese, pray that I, and all the friends of the House of Affirmation, may have the inner peace that comes from confidence, surrender, and affirmation.

FOOTNOTES

1. A carefully crafted reproduction of "Creation" which matches the painting in both fidelity and intensity of color can be ordered from *Robbins Reproductions, Rockport, Mass. 01966* for a very moderate price. The original is at the House of Affirmation in Whitinsville, Mass. This painting is the symbol of affirmation.

2. Alexander Solzhenitsyn, *'One Word of Truth . . .'* (London: The Bodley Head, 1970).

3. Thomas Aquinas, as quoted by Etienne Gilson, *History of Christian Philosophy in the Middle Ages* (New York: Random House, Inc., 1955).

4. Josef Pieper, *About Love*, trans. Richard and Clara Winston (Chicago: Franciscan Herald Press, 1974).

5. Martin Buber, "Distance and Relation," *Psychiatry* (London: Allen and Unwin, 1957).

6. Francis MacNutt, O.P., *Healing* (Notre Dame, Indiana: Ave Maria Press, 1974).

7. Michael Scanlan, *Inner Healing: Ministering to the Human Spirit Through the Power of Prayer* (New York: Paulist Press, 1974).

8. All biblical quotations are taken from *The Jerusalem Bible* (New York: Doubleday & Company, Inc., 1966).

9. Anna Polcino, M.D., Unpublished lectures, University of Massachusetts Medical School, 1971.

10. Pieper, *About Love.*

11. Jack Dominian, *Cycles of Affirmation: Psychological Essays* (London: Darton, Longman & Todd, Ltd., 1975).

12. *Ibid.*

13. John Powell, S.J., *The Secret of Staying in Love* (Niles, Illinois: Argus Communications, 1974).

14. Grace Stricker Dawson, "To a Friend," *The Best Loved Poems of the American People* (Garden City, New York: Doubleday & Company, Inc., 1936).

15. John Dalrymple, *The Christian Affirmation* (Denville, N.J.: Dimension Books, 1971).

16. Michael Wilson, M.D., *Health Is For People* (London: Darton, Longman & Todd, Ltd., 1975).

17. Adrian Van Kaam, *The Art of Existential Counseling* (Wilkes Barre, PA: Dimension Books, 1966).

18. Charles A. Curran, *Religious Values in Counseling and Psychotherapy* (New York: Sheed and Ward, 1969).

19. C. G. Jung, *Collected Works* (London: Routledge & Kegan Paul, Ltd., 1960).

20. D. T. Suzuki, *Essentials of Zen Buddhism* (London: Rider, 1963).

21. Sri Krishna Prem, *The Yoga of the Kathopanishad* (London: Robinson & Watkins, 1962).

22. James A. Weisheipl, O.P., *Friar Thomas D'Aquino: His Life, Thought, & Works* (Garden City, N.Y.: Doubleday & Company, Inc., 1974).

23. Robert Bolt, *A Man for All Seasons* (New York: Random House, Inc., 1962).
One of the earliest and still best books concerning the difference between assertion and aggression is *Your Perfect Right: A Guide to Assertive Behavior* by Alberti and Emmons published by Impact Books, San Luis Obispo, CA 1970. Revised 1975.

24. Bernard J. Bush, *Coping: Issues of Emotional Living in an Age of Stress for Clergy and Religious* (Whitinsville, Mass.: Affirmation Books, 1976).

25. Adrian Van Kaam, "Gentleness, the Deadening of Anger, the Emergence of Anxiety," *Envoy*, Vol. XI, No. IX, 1974.

26. Marshall Bryant Hodge, *Your Fear of Love* (Garden City, N.Y.: Dolphin Books, Doubleday Company, Inc., 1967).

27. Henri J. M. Nouwen, *Out of Solitude* (Notre Dame, Indiana: Ave Maria Press, 1974).

28. From a Hallmark greeting card — 247-7.

SELECTED BIBLIOGRAPHY

Alberti, Robert E., and Emmons, Michael L. *Your Perfect Right.* San Luis Obispo, CA: Impact, 1974.

Barksdale, L. S. *Building Self-Esteem.* Idyllwild, CA: The Barksdale Foundation, 1972.

Buber, Martin. *I and Thou.* Translated R. G. Smith, Edinburgh: T. and T. Clark, 1937.

Bush, Bernard J. *Coping: Issues of Emotional Living in An Age of Stress For Clergy and Religious.* Whitinsville, MA: Affirmation Books, 1976.

Colson, Charles W. *Born Again.* Lincoln, VA: Chosen Books, 1976.

Curran, Charles A. *Psychological Dynamics in Religious Living.* New York, N.Y.: Herder and Herder, 1971.
Religious Values in Counseling & Psychotherapy. New York. Sheed and Ward, Inc., 1969.

Dalrymple, John. *The Christian Affirmation.* Denville, N.J.: Dimension Books, 1971.

Dominian, Jack. *Cycles of Affirmation.* London: Darton, Longman & Todd, Ltd., 1975.

Greenwald, Dr. Jerry. *Be the Person You Were Meant to Be.* New York, N.Y.: Simon and Schuster, 1973.

Häring, Bernard. *Ethics of Manipulation.* New York, N.Y.: The Seabury Press, 1975.
Hope is the Remedy. Slough, England: St. Paul Publications, 1971.

Hodge, Marshall Bryant. *Your Fear of Love.* Garden City, N.Y.: Dolphin Books, Doubleday & Company, Inc., 1967.

Jean, Sister Gabrielle L. "Affirmation: Healing in Community", in *Review for Religious,* vol 34, n 4, 1975.

Joyce, Mary Rosera and Joyce, Robert E. *New Dynamics in Sexual Love.* Collegeville, MN: St. John's University Press, 1970.

Kane, Thomas A. *Who Controls Me?* Hicksville, N.Y.: Exposition Press, 1974.

Laing, R. D. *Self And Others.* New York, N.Y.: Pantheon Books, Random House, 1961.

Lepp, Ignace. *Love Builds Mankind.* Denville, N. J.: Dimension Books, 1971.

MacNutt, O.P., Francis. *Healing.* Notre Dame, Ind.: Ave Maria Press, 1974.

Marcel, Gabriel. *The Philosophy of Existentialism.* Secaucus, N.J.: Citadel Press, 1961.

Nouwen, Henri J.M. *Out of Solitude.* Notre Dame, Ind.: Ave Maria Press, 1974.

Pieper, Josef. *About Love*. Trans. Richard and Clara Winston, Chicago, Ill.: Franciscan Herald Press, 1974.

    Guide to Thomas Aquinas. New York, N.Y.: Pantheon Books, Random House, 1972.

    In Tune With the World. New York, N.Y.: Harcourt Brace & World, Inc., 1963.

    Leisure, The Basis of Culture. Trans. Alexander Dru. New York: The New American Library (Mentor-Omega), 1963.

Polcino, Sister Anna. "Psychotheological Community", in *The Priest*, vol. 31, No. 9, 1974.

Powell, John. *The Secret of Staying in Love*. Niles, Ill.: Argus Communications, 1974.

Sanford, Agnes. *The Healing Light*. Watchung, N.J.: Charisma Books, 1972.

Scanlan, Michael. *Inner Healing*. New York, N.Y.: Paulist Press, 1974.

Simon, O.C.S.O., M.D., M. Raphael. *Hammer And Fire*. New York, N.Y.: P. J. Kenedy & Sons, 1959.

Stern, E Mark and Marino, Bert G. *Psychotheology*. New York, N.Y.: Newman Press, 1970.

Wilson, Michael. *Health Is For People*. London: Darton, Longman & Todd Ltd., 1975.

Van Kaam, Adrian. *Envy And Originality*. Garden City, N.Y.: Doubleday & Company, Inc., 1972.

    In Search of Spiritual Identity. Denville, N.J.: Dimension Books, 1975.

    Spirituality And the Gentle Life. Denville, N.J.: Dimension Books, 1974.

    The Art of Existential Counseling. Wilkes-Barre, PA.: Dimension Books, 1966.

Von Hildebrand, Dietrich. *The Art of Living*. Chicago, Ill.: Franciscan Herald Press, 1962.

    The Sacred Heart: An Analysis of Human and Divine Affectivity. Dublin: Helicon Press, 1965.